Escape from the Land of the Hungry Ghosts

...about chaos, stress, and pain ... and the secrets to finding the way out.

Kathryn Bedard

All rights reserved. This book or any portion thereof may not be reproduced or used in any manner whatsoever without the express written permission of the publisher except for the use of brief quotations in a book review.

Printed in the United States of America

First Printing, 2014
Copyright © 2014 Kathryn Bedard. All rights reserved.
ISBN 978-1-304-81316-9

Lulu Enterprises, Inc.
3101 Hillsborough Street
Raleigh, NC 27607
919-459-5858
USA.
www.lulu.com

FORWARD

Escape from the Land of the Hungry Ghosts

With a common-sense way of blending age-old spiritual techniques into new perspectives, and pairing that blend with techniques for behavioral change, Kathi takes her lifetime of experience with the eastern arts, her knowledge as a mental health and addiction clinician, her knowledge of Twelve Step Recovery, and weaves them all together into a book that helps people access personal growth in a new and exciting way.

But: this book is not just for 12 Step Program members! Kathi sees principles embedded within the stress and chaos of all of our daily lives. Principles equal values, and values allow us to enter into deeper or newer aspects of ourselves, to embrace spirituality and serenity in more complete ways. *Pair your stress levels, your relationship and job issues, to the behaviors and attitudes found within each of these chapters, and you will find that the pain and stress of living life has much in common with the pain and stress of learning to recover.* It's all about being human, seeking meaning and purpose, and wanting a better way.

This book is straightforward about our ability to make a choice to bring serenity to the issues and chaos of life. Meditations and visualizations on these pages will push you to reach outside of yourself, connecting with nature and your surroundings. In this way, we come to understand that meditation is not just something that one does quietly tucked away in a dark room listening to sweet music. It is a living practice that can be developed and used to strip away the mundane of the day-to-day, and help one peek behind the thin veil that often covers our relationship with the divine. I always thought meditation was the practice of quieting and emptying one's mind - something I could never do! So, mediation became a place of frustration, and I walked away from it discouraged and confused. Kathi helped me to understand that the mind, like the heart, is never quiet. She helped me to understand how meditation helps us focus and listen through the clutter of our busy thoughts. Meditation should be done throughout and within the everyday world in which we live.

We don't often think of the 12 steps as a powerful clinical tool that has direct and lasting impact on behavioral change. This book offers practical ways to create structure and order through the use of progressive stress management techniques, while allowing the reader to understand the complex workings of the 12 steps in creating recovery. In these pages, we come to understand the stress, behaviors, attitudes, and feelings that we face, and how the steps can be used to resolve our issues in a systematic way. The book invites and leads the reader through exploration of the transformative power of the 12 steps, and offers enhancement of each step through the progressive use of meditation as gateway: not only into deeper parts of the mind, but also as doorway through which we can step into, interact with, and see our world in a very different way. The exercises in this book are not just random: they are designed to relieve stress and issues in a systematic and progressive fashion. The beginner in recovery will find it helpful to set up a practice of meditation to supplement changes as they occur. The old-timer in recovery will take their program deeper and see the Twelve Steps in different and fuller ways through the spirituality found in meditation. Clinicians will find this book an invaluable and educational treatment asset!

Meditation is about listening; listen to the words in this book, use the visualizations, let Kathi walk you into deeper and more intimate relationship with your life. This book is one of her gifts to all of us.

-Craig Nakken

Craig M. Nakken, MSW, CCDP, LCSW, LMFT, is a renowned author, lecturer, trainer, and family therapist specializing in the treatment of addiction. With over twenty years of experience in the areas of addiction and recovery, he presently has a private therapy practice in St. Paul, Minnesota. He has authored the following books through Hazelton:
The Addictive Personality
Reclaim Your Family From Addiction
Reclaim Your Family from Addiction Workbook
How Families Recover Love and Meaning
Men's Issues in Recovery
Finding Your Moral Compass
...and more!

Acknowledgements

T'was Grace that taught my heart to fear; and Grace, my fears relieved.
How precious did that Grace appear the hour I first believed?
-John Newton

This book is for:

Craig... It was his idea. Were it not for being led to a place where he was needed, he probably would have written it. You have enriched my life beyond words. You have a gentle spirit, and, like so many of us, learned to be so after feeling fractured, lost and alone. We are born to Divinity. But not all of us stay in it. Thank you for all you have given to me.

... my mother, who showed me at a very young age what meditation and eastern arts were all about. Wish you were here to see all that you have given me, and how well it works – if I work it.

... the men with whom I worked at the forensic hospital. You taught me so much about what one day at a time really means.

... most of all, for Charlie. We have danced with the hungry ghosts. You touch my soul with so much laughter. You held me gently in the palm of your hand and gave me shelter. I am forever in your debt. I'll let Jim Croce speak my gratitude for me: "If I could save time in a bottle..."

About Hungry Ghosts

There are many legends about Hungry Ghosts, and they go by many names. They are Pita or Yidak in Tibetan, Preta in Sanskrit. In China, sometimes the words E Gui and Gaki are used, in Japan: Gaki. But all of those labels apply to unfortunate souls who are condemned to suffer; filled with remorse and shame for actions in their human life.

According to Chinese legend, if we have committed sins of greed and excess; if we have taken from others without giving during our lifetime, if we have no compassion; when we die, we will be condemned to the Realm of the Hungry Ghosts, where we spend eternity stuck - wandering endlessly.

Those who stay in the Realm of the Hungry Ghosts are doomed to haunt places of excess and abundance, like kitchens, banks, gambling establishments, bakeries, and restaurants. Hungry ghosts - gaki - have a tiny mouth, too small for eating or drinking, and have a huge and hungry potbelly they can never fill. The gaki are tormented by insatiable hunger, thirst, and cravings forever. One is too many and 1,000 will never be enough.

In China it is believed that these poor spirits should be treated with compassion and gentleness.

A Note From The Author

"Be careful what you ask for: you just might get it."

This book pairs meditation to develop insight and stress reduction with information from the 12 steps, and techniques from clinical treatment to provide accelerated growth and change for individuals who are trying to incorporate more spirituality and serenity into their lives. It was born from many years of working with people who had addictions, mental health issues, stress and pain.

As I wrote this book I enlisted the help of others. I know how to meditate, and over the years I have watched meditation transform my life, and the lives of so many hurting and frightened individuals who wanted to learn how to create peace in their hearts and minds. I know how to lead groups and individuals in guided imagery, but that doesn't make explaining it on paper so others can do it an easy task, so I asked people to read it and let me know how to best make sense of it for beginners. My helpers told me that people would also want information to help them to believe or understand from real life experience that what I offer on these pages really works. They told me to tell about my journey so that people can understand that these techniques are real, that they do become a lifestyle, and once they *are* a lifestyle, these techniques can exert powerful influence. I offer information here about my wonderful teachers, and what they gave to me in effort to give you hope and understanding.

As I look back on my life, it seems that so many things that seemed random were not – almost as if the training I was going through was not just because I enjoyed Eastern techniques, but because there was something outside of me pushing me in that direction. My journey follows:

When I was about 5, my mother parked me in front of the television as a distraction. She was trying to get me to eat something I didn't like, and figured I wouldn't notice I was eating if I was in a trance watching something entertaining. Her plan backfired: the show had men in long flowing robes, with swords, doing a magical dance (Shaolin monks in a sword fight.) It was simply beautiful. I set down my food and stared. I was mesmerized. When Mom came into the room to check on me I pointed at the television and said: "I want to learn how to do that!" Bless her heart, she tried, but there were no Kung Fu schools in America when I was 5. She tried enrolling me in Ballet classes. No good.

When I was about 12, I was introduced to a wonderful yoga and meditation teacher from the Punjabi Province in India. She was amazingly capable of teaching eastern philosophy and technique to westerners, and had so much to give. She didn't have flowing robes or a sword, but she had a sweet spirit, and something about her wise and gentle eyes drew me in. I feel the touch of her gentle soul to this day. I learned an ancient style of yoga and meditation that was brought across the Himalayans from India to China in about 527 AD by a monk named Bodhidharma. By the time I was 17, I was actively teaching meditation and this ancient style of Hindu yoga. It fed my body and mind well, but for some reason it didn't get into my heart – my spirit. Something was missing. Those Kung Fu masters were still dancing in the back of my mind...

Still without the availability of a Kung Fu school, I found Shotokan Karate in the mid 1970s with a master of the style who spoke little English, had trained the Japanese military, and was all time Okinawan champion for over 30 years. It was an amazing physical workout: challenging, demanding and painful, but I loved it. He ruled with an iron fist, a wicked grin and a compassionate heart that told him just how hard he could push to develop but not break a spirit. My focus, discipline and everything I learned about the spirituality of overcoming obstacles in yoga and meditation was intensified and put to practical use. But it was so physical, that in the long run, it didn't do much for my mind. I became bored. Something was still missing.

In 1985 I got a call from someone I'd never met, who was a friend of a friend. She said: "Hey, you don't know me but I heard you've always wanted to take Kung Fu – if that's true, meet me tonight..." I met her, went to class, and immediately felt at home: it was yoga, meditation, exercise, spirituality, intellectual study, mentorship, serenity, flexibility, challenging; and taught by a man with laughing eyes and amazing movement. He flowed like water. My first class touched all of me: body, mind, spirit. Everything I had learned in all of those years in study of eastern arts crashed together into one place and began to make total and profound sense. In that first class, they told me a story about the history of the development of Kung Fu: an Indian monk named Bodhidharma brought techniques to the Shaolin temple in China, and even though the techniques were yoga and meditation, they set the foundation and basis for this style of Kung Fu (...coincidence?) And to really put the icing on the cake there were long flowing robes, swords and beautiful (but deadly) dances to learn.

To this day I still practice. It is the place in my life where I am so in tune with my own spirit: no worries, no ego no thought. I can simply allow instinct to take over. It is a profound, spiritual state that animals live in for most of their lives; the state we refer to when we say: "...when the dancer becomes the dance." It is a divine place of no worry, no time. It feels ancient, connected to complete joy and peace, and beyond mere words. Those men in flowing robes that I carried inside of my head since the age of 5 can now be conjured up at a moment's notice, and they manifest their wisdom in and through me. I am truly blessed.

All of that is how I learned the techniques that I gave to you here, and how it all became woven into the beautiful tapestry of my journey through life so far. I always knew it all worked, if I worked it. But there was one event that made me realize that there really is a higher purpose at work in my life, and that higher purpose was also connected to everything I ever learned, and the wonderful people who taught me. It was, in fact, as if my entire life was spent training for one specific purpose:

On September 11, 2001, following the attacks on the World Trade Center, I was asked to coordinate the logistics to take family members of those who died at World Trade, survivors who were in the buildings, and responders into the damage zone where they could mourn, construct monuments to their lost ones and grieve. Each day I accompanied 200 plus people into the damage zone. I used the techniques I was taught to try to bring peace to my body, mind and spirit (heart,) and hopefully to those around me. For 3 months I worked 12 – 16 hour days, 7 days a week, without a day off, trying to hold together people torn by so much pain. I watched over the volunteers who arrived each day, and their reactions, and tried to give them strength. I had to coordinate a job with so much detail that it was simply mind boggling... Through it all I found myself practicing meditation, breathing, and the types of mental images that we need to practice to really have a positive and calm outlook and attitude.

To this day I carry the weight of that experience in my heart: the smells, the sounds, the visuals. I could never put into words how stressful, exhausting, devastating that job was. But, it was also the most beautiful, honorable, spiritual thing I could ever have done. I am so blessed to have been chosen for that work. Humans are magnificent. The depth of compassion and gentleness of humans is something that I saw to extremes. Everything I ever learned about eastern arts was tested to the limit. I am living proof that when life doesn't give you what you think you are able to deal with:

- Meditation can change your thought process, and the energy that you put out to others. People constantly remarked about how calm I looked at World Trade. I felt completely undone, falling apart. But "completely undone" for a body who has meditated for over 40 years is a very different state than a "normal" body. I was initially surprised when people I didn't even know approached me and simply leaned on me. They invariably would say something like: "I want your energy."
- We work hard to hold onto stress – we go after it with a vengeance. We need to work on holding onto calm, and cultivate it with as much enthusiasm as we put into being stressed and unhappy. Happy or sad, our emotions are a choice that we make.
- Breathing is a magical device that anyone can learn, anyone can use – any time, any place. If we invest a few minutes a day for a couple of months we can impact our stress and our outlook on life enormously. Breathing is a coping skill that can help a person through devastating levels of stress.
- Meditation teaches us that service to others, connections to spirit and divine energy, and the stubborn pursuit of serenity are goals to strive for. My momma used to say:
"Missy, your life will keep going on with or without you. Do you want to look back some day and wonder if it could have been more fun? If we didn't have unhappiness, then joy wouldn't be as much fun, right? Without the fussing, noise and fight we would never know the sweet relief of peace and

quiet. Be determined each and every day not to be a member of the Grump family."

Without knowing it, momma knew a lot about meditation.

What a gift meditation can be. It works if you work it. I wish you peace!

-Kathi

ESCAPE FROM THE LAND OF THE HUNGRY GHOSTS

Whenever we embark on a growth process or recovery journey, it has something to do with being unsatisfied, or unfulfilled with what we have in the present; we are filled with fear, anger and pain. In some cases, we may want a change because we see serenity in others and want it for ourselves. And we become upset because we don't know how or where to start. We don't know who we are; we don't know how to fit in, and are looking for meaning and purpose. We are haunted by a hungry ghost inside of us – filled with longing – wanting what we don't have. We tend to see serenity as a thing that is outside of our self, not as something that we hold hostage deep inside of self. Serenity is within us all, and as long as we keep wanting, we will never have.

If you are reading this book, it is fair to assume that you know about, or have visited the land of the hungry ghosts. We all know about it. We've all been there on some level, and came to know it for different reasons:

- Most of us have wondered about the power that is addiction, compulsive behaviors, destructive habits, and the darkness inside of us that could cause us to abandon those we love, our careers; and our bodies, minds and spirits.
- If we live in a stress filled lifestyle, are workaholics, are on the verge of feeling burned out and exhausted, we are getting a glimpse of a dry desolate place without peace, with strained or almost non-existent relationships, feeling as if we will never be able to fill up the black hole of wanting that is inside of us.
- Some of us have seen the land of hungry ghosts from afar as we saw what a devastating illness like addiction can do to a friend or family member.

- Some of us have vacationed in the land of hungry ghosts, and perhaps even began to know the heartbreak of seeing other spirits die from an excess they could not control, before they decided that there was a better place.

Here's the thing about the land of hungry ghosts: all the while we are there, we see people on the other side of the fence who seem to have a secret for meaning and purpose. Even though we don't like the neighborhood in hungry ghost land, some of us leave our belongings and loved ones and move into that land - not consciously or willingly - but we take up residence in that restless place full of wanting, fear and pain. We become ghosts longing for the way out, wishing our lifestyle and circumstances had been different. We live there haunted by our deeds, yet we attack or run from people who try to show us where the gate is. Once you've been a ghost for a while, being haunted and haunting is all that you know.

In China, July 31 through August 30 is the time to celebrate the gaki. On the July 31, it is said that the gates of Hell unlock. A Feast for the Hungry Ghosts is held, and during that feast, the gaki are able to come through the gate to walk again with the living as honored guests: to eat and drink as "normal" people do. Families will set places at the table, and burn offerings for lost loved ones, to appease their restless souls. Offerings are also made for the poor spirits who have no family.

Perhaps that's also how 12 step programs work: the gate of Hell is unlocked, and opens into a waiting room full of people, all of whom have escaped the land of the hungry ghosts. As a ghost walks through, they are welcomed to walk among the living, and encouraged to keep coming back. There is promise of a "normal" life. The ghosts who wander into the rooms witness a land where there is serenity, where things seem to work out well, where the eyes of others glimmer with a spark of understanding, acceptance, compassion, connection, spirituality, meaning and purpose. That understanding and compassion appeases something deep inside. If a ghost can manage to hide out in these rooms long enough, sometimes, when the gate closes again, they remain on the side of the living.

THE SECRET TO STICKING TO SELF IMPROVEMENT: WHY DOES IT HAVE TO BE SO HARD?

Sometimes when we start a personal growth program, we simply accept it at face value, without analyzing how it works, what the impact may be, and what it does to and for us. If we don't know what it is, and what it does; then how do we know what to expect? Understanding how we get stressed, how we develop spiritually, and how the information in this book weaves it all together can help with insight and understanding of the frustration that seems to plague us when we try to grow and change.

In the beginning section, we will look at how and why we find ourselves in places of turmoil. We will be a bit analytical and discuss how humans use their brains so you will be better able to have understanding and success when we get to the working part. We will discuss development of spirituality, and compare it to how we use our brains so that you can understand how the things that happened as you grew up may have had an impact on your ability to feel spiritual now, and understand your thought process and why it sometimes seems so hard. We will discuss how the use of tools like the 12 steps and meditation will equip us to not only frame our frustrations differently, and interact with our world and our self in a more positive manner, but actually become a life management guide that will keep us on the right track.

If we understand things we can change them.

BEING ANALYTICAL

12 STEPS?
Bill Wilson, the primary author of Alcoholics Anonymous and the Twelve Traditions, developed activities that any individual could use toward spiritual growth and development. He wove together philosophy, psychology, rules of community and spirituality into a complete lifestyle approach that has saved millions of people from the land of hungry ghosts. The way in which the 12 steps came to be, and how they work is nothing short of magical. They also work on any type of issue imaginable, and can be combined beautifully with many other interventions or techniques.

An interesting thing occurs when we look at the 12 steps through different lenses:
- A person who is involved in Eastern philosophy and techniques like yoga, meditation, martial arts can see a direct segmentation of the steps by body – mind – spirit, meaning that the steps work on, and provide development in those areas in a distinct and progressive fashion. We need to target all areas of self to make meaningful and lasting impact.
- A person who is involved in clinical work can see a direct impact on behavior that is also progressive. The steps are a systematic life management plan that offers structure, connection, persuasive and supportive levels of change that will help us to reorganize our thinking, responses and reactions to situations.
- An educator/trainer can see a comprehensive behavioral coaching plan, designed to provide insight, understanding and basic skills – really a self-parenting program.

The 12 steps are beautiful tools for learning to live life in compassionate joy and serenity. The 12 steps also teach us that what we seek is already ours.

MEDITATION?

Meditation, like the steps, is so versatile it can be used any time, any place, and needs no special equipment that drains our pocket book. From trying to learn to dance, to overcoming phobia and pain, to eliminating stress in our life, meditation is a weapon that can slay huge dragons. Meditation makes serenity a tangible thing. It can bring us to a different outlook, a different way of living; if we work on it daily.

There are hundreds of types of meditation, and millions of ways to use it. It isn't just for some people, it's for everyone. Like the 12 steps, meditation focuses on responsibility for self, spiritual development, service orientation, and serenity. To incorporate meditation into life, one has to be willing to surrender ego, admit they need a Higher Power to give their stress to, become willing to accept their flaws, look deep inside and change the behavior and thought processes that are counterproductive. Meditation is a series of steps toward ongoing spiritual development and growth. Sound familiar? It works if you work it!

Meditation coupled with understanding the techniques used in the 12 steps becomes a vehicle to look inward and discover that the ghost is actually a beautiful, creative, extraordinary being who can accept life in the present, forget the past, let go of the need to control the future, and be strong enough to smile in the face of chaos.

THE BODY-MIND-SPIRIT CONNECTION

We are one human, existing in three states of being: the body filters the world through sensations, the mind through thoughts and feelings, and the spirit through wisdom. Ideally, all three of our realms of existence – body, mind and spirit - should work in harmony. When one of those states is out of whack due to a stressor, all three participate in prolonging the dysfunction:

- The body desperately tries to maintain survival by secreting fight or flight hormones which only serve to keep us in a state of emergency.
- The mind kicks into high gear because there is an emergency, sorting through internal files at a rapid rate – providing us with racing dialogues of basically useless information that we become too overwhelmed to use.
- The spirit remains quietly waiting in that place of peace that we can't find because our thoughts are racing and our bodies are in a fear state.

Re-connecting the body, mind and spirit is the key to eliminating stress, changing negativity, creating peace on purpose, and having what many refer to as living in harmony with our true selves; with understanding of meaning and purpose.

ORIGINS OF GHOSTS

PHYSICAL ME, AND HOW I GOT STRESSED
When we were just a fertilized egg, we began to subdivide and organize into a human. Cells collected to form our spinal cord and brain stem. The brain stem is the part of our brain that is primitive and instinctive. It senses all of the other creatures around us, and based on the smells, body language and biorhythms of those other creatures; it tells us if they are friendly or dangerous. The brain stem is in charge of physical things: automatic, predictable, and repetitive (ritualistic) functions like breathing, digestion, preserving balance, life and safety. It has no language, no rationality. One reason we come into this world screaming is that our brain that had not yet developed a thought process. As we burst into the world, that small, warm, fluid environment in mommy's tummy suddenly becomes cold, bright, loud, and expansive. Screaming is about all the brain can do to tell the little body that something is

horribly out of balance. That scream is also a primitive survival mechanism: the high pitched wail of an infant is supposed to cause a reaction in the brain stems of the nearby adults of the species, resulting in a protective response. Babies are survival machines. They interact with the world through reflexes: babies suck on anything in their mouths. Tiny fingers wrap around anything that touches their palm. Smell differentiates mom from the family dog or a random stranger.

From birth, we are spiritual in a very innocent and pure sense: we have a need to bond, a basic instinct that pushes us toward community, sharing and love: survival in numbers. Spirituality of babies is evident in laughter, snuggling closeness, innocence and purity, reaching toward others, and warm reactions to those who are familiar. Babies only live in the moment: now. There is no judgment. There is no worry clouding innocent baby thoughts: they trust and give unconditionally and without suspicion. *But* as we develop relationships with everything and everyone in our world, we do what is called "individuation:" the separation of me from the outside world. We discover that our fingers are different from the slats of our crib; our skin is different from our clothes and blankets. The earliest things we store in our brain files are about soft and warm, vs. harsh and cold, and we store information about "ME" – the beginning of our identity. As we individuate we also sort out everything outside of self: NOT ME and WE. NOT ME can include toys, pets, people - the beginning of our understanding of family, but WE means that others can be used to meet our needs. Babies are not at a point where there is a conscious give and take in a relationship: they give out of instinct, not through thought. Babies are just not capable of thinking: "As soon as I see Mom I'll give her a hug, she looked sad this morning."

WHY SELF IMPROVEMENT IS SO HARD
As we grow up, we typically notice that stress has infiltrated our life when we see changes in the body such as: headaches, stiff

neck and shoulders, tight jaw, anxiety attacks, sleeplessness, and a host of other adrenaline related symptoms. We tend to minimize all of those signals from our body as minor annoyances, but as the mind begins to experience overload, we disconnect: from community, work, friends, family, and ultimately from our own body, mind and spirit; and that disconnect happens in that order:

- the disconnect from the body occurs as we deny those subtle symptoms of stress.
- the disconnect from the mind occurs after stress has accumulated and we being burning out, no longer able to think clearly. We allow numbness to take over so that we no longer hurt so much or have to think.
- the disconnect from the spirit occurs when we progress from burnout to ballistic and overwhelming stress, and see no way out. When this happens we allow the brain stem to completely take over - telling us danger is everywhere - it is time to hide.

Under stress, our brain stem is creating symptoms and behaviors through high adrenaline levels to tell us the world is not balanced or safe. It has sensed danger and manufactured fight-or-fight response. Brain stem can't speak because it has no language. It doesn't turn to others because it is only designed to govern the human that owns it. It is ME centered.   No matter how old we are, if we are feeling alone and vulnerable, our brain stem wakes up, triggering survival mode. Because this part of the brain is so concrete, so concerned with survival and balance, any attempt to modify what it is doing is met with high resistance to change. Think of it this way: if we were cave men in the wild, if we stopped to ponder the ramifications of the situation we were in, the predator would get us, so we trust our brain stem to guide us to safety. In early sobriety, in times of high stress, we are operating in emergency survival mode, and unless we are stopped by an outside force, we will resist efforts to change.

Addiction is also ME centered. Essentially, for our brain, being in the high stress of early sobriety is a lot like being an infant: we don't make connections beyond what hurts and what doesn't, and everything is scary – yet we don't seem to have the skills to sort it out or fix it. Because addiction and stress are both very hard on relationships, many people caught in stress and early sobriety think that they have no one left to turn to, or think that they are not capable of asking for help. Anxiety and stress may have been useful for cavemen who led challenging and dangerous lives, but for someone trying to develop spiritually, or simply lead a happy, peaceful life, the chemical state of an anxious body keeps us stuck as that lone wolf simply trying to survive, seeing others as a threat, not knowing how to reach out to others without growling threats and yelping in pain.

WHAT CAN THE 12 STEPS AND MEDITATION DO FOR MY BRAIN STEM?
The first three of the 12 steps are a mechanism to create a brain stem over ride, and allow us to see that there is a path open in front of us. If we choose to walk it. And that path will lead to a better land. These beginning steps are working to sort out and impact the physical environment by diminishing chaos through specific coping skills: both internal and external.

The first three steps are about control issues; how we landed in our current state of unhappiness:
- The first step tells us that we have found ourselves in an intolerable situation because we are out of control, and furthermore: control is a myth.
- Someone in an intolerable situation is a person alone, frightened, with racing thoughts – a desperate, sad, hungry ghost, running from pain, who is looking for answers to the

questions 'why?' and 'how?' Step one teaches that disorganized person who is running on adrenaline, not really capable of making decisions, that they aren't alone, that others have been there, and are willing to pass along their secrets and wisdom.
- As we move to step two and three, we are told that if we reach out, life will become more orderly (sane.) These three steps are taking our confused brain stem by the hand, leading it to a safe place. We are being provided with reinforcement and repetition: 'Come with me, yes, it's out of control, it's okay, we've all been there. Let something else regulate your world while you rest awhile. Let go of it all, and balance will occur.'

A BIT ABOUT ANXIETY ATTACKS
It's important for people with stress, and especially for people in early recovery to understand anxiety attacks. Most people who have anxiety attacks are high achievers, are ambitious, and intelligent. They give 110%. The bright side of having anxiety attacks is: you are a wonderful person who cares passionately about many, many things. Anxiety attacks can also come from: Diabetes, hypoglycemia, hypertension, puberty, menopause, pregnancy, lack of aerobic exercise, poor diet/nutritional imbalances, too much coffee, medications, herbal supplements, diet products, alcoholism, drug addiction and a host of other things. Anxiety and panic may be physical, may be emotional, but it can be treated, and it does not have to continue to rule your life. Once you really understand the process you are going through, and can stop worrying about it, the anxiety will lessen. *The most crucial part of overcoming anxiety attacks is first, and foremost: if you have anxiety or panic, and have not yet seen your doctor – do so now!*

If we were cave men in the wild, the chemical composition of stress hormones puts us in the physical state that would be needed to run from or escape a predator, so a state of anxiety was very useful for cave men with challenging and dangerous lives. When humans become chronically anxious, our fight or flight response becomes confused due to the high levels of adrenaline that we have created with worry, so instinctive reaction is more easily triggered. Once our instinctive survival mode is triggered and continues on a regular basis, we begin to think in negative terms, and we begin to feel "badly." If we are chronically anxious at work, we may begin to form negative connections with the work place, because that is where we feel bad. We may also begin to associate the "bad feelings" with locations we are in when we have an anxiety or panic attack, hence they become "bad places." Eventually just going outside may be a fearful concept. Simplified, the physical chain of events happens like this:

ONE: Think about how you feel when someone sneaks up behind you and says "BOO!": The initial reaction is to have a startle response — jump at the sound. The brain cannot analyze when startled; it simply perceives in a split second that something is out of whack, and aggressively attempts to manage the situation by calculating skin temperature, blood pressure, respiration, muscle tension and the levels of many chemicals in our system.

TWO: The very first thing a body does in response to the startle is tighten the abdominal muscles: an instinctive and primitive physical reaction that humans and other animals are hard wired to have to protect vital organs in case of attack. That spasm sends a message to the brain that danger is imminent: "prepare to either fight or run."

THREE: We retreat into a primitive and instinctive part of our brain. Thoughts don't turn to others for help because thinking would delay response time and place the self in greater threat. We become primitive, animalistic in the sense that we are reacting to our body: our own internal chemical composition.

FOUR: To prepare the body for quick and frenetic activity, we gasp. The breath becomes shallow and rapid, and located high

in the chest. This breathing pattern is another primitive signal; we only pant when we move fast or exert ourselves in some way. The brain reads muscle tightness and shallow rapid breathing as a request for more adrenaline, and it responds by delivering more. We begin to feel like the tiny mouse that skitters in several different directions when the log he was hiding under has been removed. With all of that adrenaline in our system our hands begin to tremble, we become "jittery."
FIVE: The cycle becomes stress when we repeatedly trigger additional adrenaline through negative thoughts and worrying over being worried. Essentially we manufacture more anxiety, which makes us feel more negative, and compounds our anxiety.

The most important thing to remember about your response to negativity is that it spurs your brain into thinking you are in danger, which results in body chemistry geared for rapid activity. If we keep running fast inside, we will eventually become frazzled – we wear out.   In many cases, in conjunction with treatment with your doctor, skill building can help the anxiety to dissipate. The goal in overcoming anxiety attacks is to minimize the importance that you place on the experience. Remember two extremely important rules:
- If you can learn to laugh at it, it can no longer hurt you.
- If you had a sense of humor you would not have stress.

So – your stress level is COMPLETELY under your control. You are in charge of how anxious you want to be.

Anxiety attacks feel horrible - like the world is coming to an end. When you are having an anxiety attack, it is very difficult to think clearly, so you need tips that are simple and practical to recall no matter where you may find yourself when you suddenly feel out of control. You may want to make a little index card to write down suggestions:

1. Fear of having another attack is usually what sets up the next episode. Tell yourself firmly to *stop being afraid to be afraid* – objectively it makes no sense – you'll understand how it works if you try it.
2. Remove your ability to beat yourself up by understanding that the process is a physical chain of events. It isn't your fault. Think of it as an honor to be intimately connected to ancient cave dwellers, and to be a person who is deeply caring and passionate.
3. Give yourself permission to panic. Diminish the power your symptoms have over you. Tell yourself you will go out, have a good time, an anxiety attack or two over dinner with friends, and also laugh, share a meal, and live through the experience.
4. Death from an anxiety attack is extremely rare – despite what your brain is telling you when it happens. Repeat to yourself: "I'm having an anxiety attack – I will not die."
5. You aren't "crazy," either. Repeat to yourself: "I am having an anxiety attack, I am not losing my mind."
6. Your thoughts during an attack are irrational. Train yourself to say: "What is the worst thing that will happen to me?" and really answer the question truthfully and factually.
7. Control your breathing – hyperventilating is only telling your brain that you want MORE panic producing chemicals, and it will respond by delivering exactly what you ask for.
8. EXERCISE! Move your body, use up that adrenaline and all of that rampant energy through aerobic exercise, which will also give you more dopamine, endorphins and relaxing hormones.
9. Get a drink of water and sit down somewhere. Talk to someone.
10. Learn to meditate and do it every day.

FEAR IS A SIGNAL THAT WE NEED TO LET GO

It is possible to let go of fear and create calm in our internal and external environment, and allow the wolf inside to see that the pack means no harm, and will actually assist us in survival. This is the beginning of how the steps trigger faith and hope, along with teaching social skills for reaching out and accepting. As all of that learning develops, the hungry ghost begins to learn how to let go of fear and feel the magic and promises of these initial three steps:

- My life is a mess, but there is another way.
- There are calm, level headed people who have the peace and knowledge that I crave, and they want to help me.
- If I stop controlling, I will feel more in control.
- I feel something interestingly warm and peaceful in those rooms, and I want MORE! When I'm there I'm calm.
- If I accept that I can't control everything, I will feel free.
- If I have faith and reach out, allowing outside guidance and structure to take over, I will feel peace.
- If I practice faith, allow something instead of ME to take over, my attitude, skills and circumstances will change.
- I may still have the past – and all of its ugliness, but I will be strong enough to embrace that part of me, and still be happy.
- I need never to be alone and haunted again.

Interestingly enough, all of the things above are the premise and gifts of meditation as well: control is a myth. Trying to control will result in chaos; surrender is the pathway to peace. To accomplish this in meditation, we focus on balancing the physical: calming the body through breathing and systematic relaxation exercises, setting the tone with soothing music, low light, and quiet.

The way in which meditation impacts on the physical is by stimulating the brain stem through breathing and focusing exercises, deliberately locating and releasing the stress caught in our bodies, which directly results in taming our wild thoughts and anxieties. When the wild thoughts dissipate, the brain stem thinks the world is now calm, and changes the chemicals that it sends through our system to the chemicals that we would need to be still: dopamine, serotonin and endorphins. That furthers the calm state and allows it to continue. This is why meditations that focus on the physical realm can provide some stress relief in as little as three days. Guided images that focus on letting go, connecting to others, purging of negativity, and reframing thoughts can help to teach us how we hold on to things that are no longer useful. As the meditative techniques give us tangible feelings of calm, our adrenaline levels continue to reduce, fears begin to diminish, and we are more able to step outside of ME. Learning to reach out, ask for, and accept help is a very important thing to know, a difficult thing to do, and is key in helping us to access a higher order thought process.   In other words, inducing calm can help us to think. If we can think, we can sort it all out and make sense of it. Once it makes sense we can take action.

"I DO BELIEVE IN SPOOKS"   – Cowardly Lion
Our thinking brain is the limbic system, which wraps around the brain stem. This part of our brain filters information much like the search engine of a computer: sorting through millions of files in a Nano second, and then suggesting infinite options to explore. Over our first year of life, our job is to file away memories and information, and develop habits, and we put all of that in our limbic system. With a new born, momma touches the bottle to the baby's lips and instinctive sucking begins. During the first few months of life, the brain begins to recognize repeated patterns in the world, and forms relationships between those patterns: baby sees momma approaching with a bottle, and reaches for the bottle. We discover that food makes our empty belly feel better; screaming gets rid of wet diapers. We connect the soft skin of mom to soft blankets, to fuzzy toys, and

if all goes well, predictably and consistently, we put memories into a file called "warm and happy," and we giggle and coo, and happily reach out when we see those things. Like our brain stem, the limbic system is also primitive, so the only way our brain can communicate needs to itself and the world outside is through degrees of pain that are usually expressed in wails that mean:

My diaper is wet,
I'm hungry,
I'm afraid— hold me.

Because we are so dependent on caregivers, we are developing files in our heads with information about how NOT ME provides for trust, safety, security, consistency, rejection, love, warm, soft and predictability. If we are hungry, cold, have no nurturing, we begin to develop files with dark and scary messages inside, and our brain stem dumps distress chemicals into our bodies. At under the age of one year, we are already learning all about stress and anxiety. Because a baby cannot think beyond "ME" to understand cause and effect, fear and pain is internalized along with our growing identity, so our faith, trust and attachments in ever widening circles can be disrupted at this very young age. If we are developing files in our brain labeled "unworthy" and "unlovable," pain is attached to those messages, not thought or reasoning. Even as a baby, because we are identifying so strongly with ME, if we have too much pain we can begin to drift away from the state of innocence and spirituality that was our birthright.

Situations that we file away as a baby can be very dark memories, because they are processed without language, and are stored away as emotional reactions. Because these memories were formed so early, there is no explanation available to us, so as adults, if these memories are triggered, we go back in time to the hurt and the fear, and don't know why, or specifically what caused it. We begin to attempt to avoid things that hurt, and seek things that feel good.

Still...the lone wolf continues to do anything he can to survive.

TODDLING AND ABOUT TO BECOME A WHIPPERSNAPPER
As we grow into toddler and school age, our world becomes about making choices on our own, and being imaginative and creative. The limbic system brings language, and the ability to interact with others, and those skills evolve at a very rapid rate. Each day brings new things to learn about. Young children discover other humans of various sizes, and the concept of "we" becomes "relationships." In the limbic brain, relationships are like being in a pack or a herd. We are with others, we may have strong feelings about them, we may all be involved in doing something together, but those connections are existing alongside of others: parallel play. We don't yet have the part of our brain that understands servitude, meaning, purpose, connection, compassion and empathy. Our values are based in what we get from home and school. Children can love life, have great concepts about self, but the meaning of life has to do with becoming a fireman, the president, a shark or Tarzan—sometimes all in the same conversation. We like stories, and our ability to have faith has to do with what we see: Santa is at the mall, therefore he must exist. We are learning "good" and "bad," laughter, play and love. We begin learning more about ME by comparing ME to those who are NOT ME, and we internalize our thoughts about how strong or weak we are in comparison. We begin to seek out fun, approval, and we perform for praise. As a toddler, if we are always told that we make bad choices, if we aren't allowed to exert power in our world, we can develop shame, self-doubt and powerlessness. Our sense of being "good" and "bad" effect how much confidence we develop, how social we become as adults.

The lone wolf discovers a pack...

THERE REALLY IS A MONSTER UNDER THE BED
From about age 6 to 12, with each thing we conquer, our self-confidence, strength, capability, and belief in self grows. We are like little mad scientists: experimenting with everything, testing everything, exploring sometimes without regard to reason or safety– because we don't yet know how to reason.

Our brain now has creativity and imagination that we can turn into reality with clay, crayons and stories. We can organize groups and make up stories and games. As we grow into preteen and begin to really have our own ideas, we begin to develop the skills to operate in a material plane: to gain possessions, demonstrate our abilities at dodge ball, manipulate things around us in the environment. The material plane is a ME centered world, filled with stress and wanting, and we invent dark messages when our needs and wants are frustrated. Now the dark messages are not just feelings and sensations like they were when we were infants. The dark messages have language, and are a collection of the things we hear from parents and the humans around us, and they begin to guide ME through the world:
There is something wrong with me.
I'm different.
I'm not okay.
I'm not lovable.
I'm not worthy.
No one loves me.

These unacceptable parts of self take on a life of their own – like a monster under the bed. Because the brains of children are being rewired daily, being in prolonged states of stress can lead the brain to create too many files named 'fear.' We learn about shame when we can't escape our sense of powerlessness and we experience something that we aren't ready for, or have no support to handle. Shame leads us to believe that NOT ME is a hostile place. If we hurt too much, eventually ME becomes a hostile place as well. Our negative thoughts keep us in fear, teach us to judge, and we hurt. "BAD ME" is a trigger for the development of guilt – but because we still don't have capacity for rational reason, this guilt comes without the knowledge of what we did wrong, why we are not deserving, why we don't measure up to NOT ME. We hunger for belonging. This is a spiritual crisis: we want so much to get back to the source of innocence, comfort, warm, love, and soft but we don't know where it is, or how to get it. And wailing to have our needs met doesn't work anymore. Support and encouragement from caretakers is vital in developing pride, hope, self-confidence and the understanding that we are not an embarrassment.

While limping away through the trees, the wolf has discovered that sometimes the pack can be very cruel...

ADOLESCENCE IS SPIRITUAL
Our limbic system is where we do most of our thinking throughout later childhood and adolescence, and by now it has huge filing cabinets of information. This is one reason why the job of adolescents is to be unpredictable, emotional, passionate and reactive. The third part of our brain, which is our center for rational decision making, meaning, purpose and spirituality has not yet developed enough to regulate our behavior, but our adolescent limbic brains are becoming aware that there is a higher nature to humans: a spirit, a divine source somewhere inside that may be tapped for wisdom and innocence– the place where we find answers to the questions:
Who am I?
Why am I here?
What is the meaning of life?
Adolescence is a time for fitting in, organizing little societies of friends who think like we do, so we can continue to experiment with the world in safety while we manufacture who we are.

Because we are still thinking primarily from our limbic system, relationships are still a bit like parallel play. Intensity and intimacy get all mixed up: we meet a pretty new face and talk about the intimacy that we immediately feel; not understanding that intimacy develops in our higher brain, over time, with wisdom, give and take. Intensity is really our brain stem reacting to that pretty face.

As adolescents, we grow spiritually through testing theories, experimenting with roles, connection to others who have ideas and values that we admire. But spirituality is not clear cut because it has to do with purpose, hope, faith and other intangible things we can't pin down, hold on to or describe, and it occurs in a part of our brain that is underdeveloped until we are about 25. So everything we search for in adolescence is frustratingly out of reach. If we have support during our adolescent searching, we develop a sense of competent, independent ME, capable of developing supportive relationships. If our relationships with self and others are full of stress and pain, we leave adolescence feeling alone, isolated, without a community to belong to. If we are always running from painful interactions we may either become a loner, or chase relationships for intensity, so we will never have to worry about being too close.

BABY BRAIN NEVER GROWS UP – FEAR IS A LACK OF FAITH
Our reactions to the information in our limbic system all the way back at the age of 6 can become a trigger for emotion and turmoil throughout life. For instance: as an adult, if I am nervous about a situation, and want to avoid it, the limbic system tells the brain stem about being nervous, unsafe and alone. It then pulls related files out of the archives to clarify and reinforce the notion that we are nervous, unsafe and alone: like the time when we cried out in hunger and fear as a baby, but caretakers were abusive, and there was no relief from the hunger… and the file from the 6 year old self crying in fear; alone

and hurt by a bully... and the 15 year old that was called ugly and picked on without mercy for wearing the wrong sneakers. All of those files with negative experiences about 'nervous, unsafe and alone' trigger the brain stem to release the chemicals that we might need to cope with danger, threat and survival if we are nervous, unsafe and alone: adrenaline. Unfortunately, adrenaline compounds stress, and reinforces negative feelings. Remember, the brain stem has no language. It isn't rational. It doesn't decide: "I have to give myself serotonin, dopamine and endorphins to relax and counteract all of the information in these files, and eliminate this stress." When stressed, it says: "DANGER! Run! Hide!" ...and provides the body with precisely what it needs to accomplish safety, using the premise that if we spend time thinking and rationalizing, something will jump out of the bushes and get us. Also unfortunately, since the limbic system is a filing cabinet, the brain stem will continue to dump adrenaline until it receives information that we are safe. That information never comes because the limbic system is in overdrive pulling out files about anxiety and pain– some of which were made as a baby with no language. The information is incomplete, so the search engine goes into overdrive, the mind races with incomprehensible information and feelings, and ME feels even more anxious. The hard drive crashes.

HOW CAN THE 12 STEPS AND MEDITATION FIX MY SEARCH ENGINE?
A person who is stuck in operating from their limbic system might think in terms of "magical" faith, hope, and outside cures, as opposed to understanding that they have a role in bringing about events in their lives: "Please God, I'll do anything if you just grant my wishes..."
Through the first three of the 12 steps, the hungry ghost begins to find fulfillment in accepting that there is a path and others to lead the way; that there really is such a thing as "calm." Steps four through six of the 12 steps begin the process of taking our

searching, questioning but essentially paralyzed brain, and gives it something to think about that is productive: a real *plan* for survival that includes a structured community of others. As they continue to unfold, the 12 steps become an undoing and remaking mechanism, giving the busy brain constructive direction by introducing new files filled with new information. With new information, the brain can see that it has to take inventory of everything and make new connections.

These steps tell us with language to quit screaming and running away, and simply pick a place to start. All of the files have to be organized if the brain is going to begin to sort out the mess and begin to really plan. But because we don't yet know how to use all of this information we are in a body-mind split. Deep inside, the hungry ghost approaching steps 4 – 6 is still wailing:
I'm hungry,
I'm afraid— hold me.
There is something wrong with me.
I'm not okay.
I'm not lovable.
I'm not worthy.

"As we examine our defects of character, we will see how our faulty, negative thinking helped to keep us in the land of hungry ghosts."   - Buddha

The 12 step program at this middle stage tells us that we need to stop, danger is gone. NOW is the time to look inward at how we got ourselves into this mess, become ready to define a new life, and confront our worst enemy (ME) by spilling our guts to another person. All of that shame, guilt, remorse, evil deeds, abuse, anger, hurt, unworthiness, resentment... every dark message we have stored in our infinite filing system since birth needs sorting out, and new files need to be created. We are told that if we find our fear and pain, talk about it, and decide to let it go, the darkness will leave us, and we will see how to reach out and have a positive and serene existence. Through this behavior we learn to be strong, confident, and to take responsibility for our past, present and future. It is also here that the 12 steps begin to re-parent us, by teaching us to be our own loving caretaker.

The lone wolf can now belong to a pack, and rely on its wisdom and protection.

MEDITATION?
Out of all of the animals in the kingdom, humans have the most brain power, resulting in the most options for survival, the most opportunity for comfort and security, and the power to make mountains move if we really put our resources to it. But it is also that huge computer in our heads that causes our confusion, misery, paralysis and turmoil. Meditation is a vehicle to understand that everyone has racing thoughts. Our goal is to begin to accept things beyond our control, and deliberately seize the opportunity to sit quietly and practice acceptance. Meditation begins to teach us that the magic bullet for our problems is actually in our own brain. If we can create anxiety, we can create calm. If we are experiencing racing thoughts and chaos in our heads, we are having control issues. What better thing to do with control issues than refocus them into controlling our brains into a calm state?

STOP ALL THAT HOWLING AND CLEAN OUT THE FILING CABINET!
It is very important to understand that when we focus on something, it becomes all important. That sounds obvious, but when we dredge up all of those dark thoughts and deeds, we disorganize, we trigger survival mode – which can result in us becoming somewhat incapable of rationality. Even if we have been working a solid spiritual program for 50 years, if we decide to go back to redo steps, it would be 'normal' to see anxiety, self-centered thoughts, irritability and a host of other stress related symptoms emerge, because as we re-examine old

thoughts, patterns and attitudes, the brain stem responds to our thoughts, taking us back to that primitive place of a 4 year old who is convinced that there is a monster under the bed (there is – the monster is in those dark thoughts!)

Tools like meditation are good to have at a time when we are triggering our own stress and working through difficult issues. Like the 12 steps, meditation tells us that we need to stop; we invented the danger – stop and look inward at how we got ourselves into this mess, become ready to define a new life, and confront our worst enemy (ME.) As we learn to look inward quietly, we will find our desire to not let go of the things that are familiar, our desire to complicate the process, our desire to impose our will, and our need to be afraid of something that we cannot understand or change. Self exploration (inventory) forces us to look at self and grow. If we focus on calm, calm takes on great importance: it grows and takes over our life; just as anxiety once did. Meditation teaches us how to compassionately overcome stress, and those dark messages in our heads by minimizing the importance that you place on the experience:
- If you can learn to laugh at it, it can no longer hurt you.
- If you had a sense of humor you would not have stress.
- My thoughts will be there whether I am frustrated or not, so I might as well practice acceptance, tolerance, patience, put on a smile, and begin to stop fighting and controlling.

When we combine the inward exploration of meditation with relaxation techniques, we create the ability to soul-search with calmness and confidence: the brain stem thinks that we are in deep relaxation, or sleep state, and gives us serotonin, dopamine, endorphins to elevate our mood and keep us relaxed; even when things get tough. These chemicals have a direct impact on the thought process as well – just as adrenaline has a side effect of negative thought patterns; relaxation hormones have a side effect of positivity. We will no longer have a need to rapidly search through brain files when there is no emergency state, we can sit and reflect on how good we feel. If we purge the brain files that are full of negativity, and replace them with positive, we increase our chances of remaining in a good space. Through meditation, as we learn to relax, our breaths become longer, less hurried. Thoughts slow down until it seems like we are not thinking at all.

SPIRITUAL ME

HAUNTED BY MISTAKES
Sometimes we get stuck in doing the same thing over, and over, and getting the same results; yet we don't give up that pattern. None of us are perfect. Our parents weren't perfect, and they didn't raise perfect children. Mistakes are rooted in the past, and keep us stuck there. As long as we keep concentrating on what we have done wrong, we continue to pay for it every waking day. If we concentrate so hard on feeling bad for our mistakes, we never really take action to accept responsibility; never get a chance to make amends, never learn a new way – we sit in self-pity and wonder why life is so hard. You have already paid enough for your mistakes: you have felt the pain, guilt and remorse from your actions – probably for years. Once we develop the skills to manufacture serenity in our life, we begin to understand that mistakes are sacred, spiritual events and exciting opportunities.

When we make mistakes, our internal voice nags at us for not being perfect and that voice begins to shape our view of self, beginning way back at the ages of toilet training. Over time, we turn into our own executioner, and ME is the worst executioner ever. If we tend to punish our self too much, we may also become fearful: afraid to take risks, afraid of relationships, afraid to take action – so we get stuck, and any additional lack of success is reason for additional self-loathing. That makes growth and change difficult: why change if it isn't worth it? (If ME isn't worth it.) If we can become our worst punisher, we can also become our best supporter. You deserve a joyful life! You can reprogram your brain; teach it more options and choices for the future.

Falling flat on our face is a learning opportunity. My momma used to tell us: "Learn to enjoy humiliation – it takes the surprise out of it the next time it happens." The way we come to the point of being able to understand negative events as opportunities to embrace for knowledge, is to understand a few things about being "wrong:"

- We act based on the best information and skills we have in the moment; it is only after the dust settles that we realize that we don't like the outcome. If we don't know *how*, we can't *do* differently.
- We may tell our self: "But I know better... I should have..." Knowing and being able to call up the reasoning power when you need it are two different things. In the split second of time when we make a decision we may not be in a frame of mind where rationality, reason and weighing all of the pros and cons are possible.
- Our brain is complex. From our discussions up to now, you realize that you use one area of your brain to stay alive and breathing, another to store information, and a third for experiencing spirituality, meaning and purpose. Under pressure, we are flying blind: sorting through information to find the best solution, reacting to that information, and just trying to keep our head above water. At that point we aren't able to incorporate as many values, spiritual principles and rationality as we might like, because when humans become emotional, logic and reason generally go out the window. It doesn't make you "bad." It makes you human, and gives you plenty of fuel for growth and change.

- Negative self talk is a warning sign. Anything we dwell on becomes very important. If we dwell on our mistakes, we eventually become a walking mistake. If we dwell on the facts that we may make mistakes, but we also have great attributes: caring deeply, passion, energy, creativity, intelligence – all of those things will become more and more important until they overshadow our shortcomings.
- Sometimes we fight against people and situations because we care deeply. Rather than reacting in anger and resentment, we can learn to stop, recognize how passionate and caring we really are, and reframe our thoughts and actions.
- To move on, we need to first forgive our self for being imperfect. It's funny how easy it is to dislike our self, but self-love can be so difficult, because many of us are so used to beating our self up on a regular basis.
- Mistakes are full of judgment. Judgment of self and others might just be one of the biggest obstacles to really seeing the joy that surrounds us. As long as we allow ourselves to remain in a state of judging the mistakes of self and others, we will remain haunted.

NO MORE HAUNTING.
Our spirituality develops in a part of our brain called the Neo-cortex, which is wrapped around the outside surface of the brain. It doesn't really develop fully until we are in our mid-twenties, about the time when the turmoil of adolescence winds down, and we leave schooling for the work world. This is the part of the brain that deals with voluntary movement, operational thinking, planning, reasoning, language, speech and writing; where free will resides, and smart decisions are made. This part of our brain sets us apart from the rest of the animal kingdom, because it is in this part of our brain that we can have that "AH HA!" experience: an epiphany. When we use this section of our brain we can have deliberate and forward

thinking, and tribal communication – like planning a raid of the neighboring community. Now there is not only safety in numbers, and ability to act as a group, but there is cunning, manipulation and power seeking that is deliberate and calculated, and most importantly, designed as part of a complex plan. With our Neo-cortex, we can develop intimacy, desire to serve others, meaning and purpose, spiritual connections, morals and values, and we begin to live by them more consistently.

Spirituality is the silver bullet that destroys self-centeredness. We choose to feel love, hate, anger, joy. When we feel good inside, others are drawn to us because they want that positive energy. When we feel bad, and have a negative, stress filled outlook, we will attract energy that is negative. Our interactions with others are a reflection of our relationship with our self: if we are unhappy we will have little sense of humor left to give to others. (Whenever we are having a hard time in any relationship, it is because we are fighting with our self.)   No matter what it may be now, relationships can be completely turned around if we embrace the positives that spirit has to offer.

"GOD NEVER GIVES YOU MORE THAN YOU CAN HANDLE"
The 12 steps are amazing life changing tools designed to bring a person from the depth of despair as a haunted, hungry ghost, toward building values, creating a community, and a spiritual lifestyle. The first three of the 12 steps worked on creating a quieter, calmer atmosphere – the physical nature of stress and living, and along with that appeasing our frazzled brain stem. The second three began the process of pushing the mind in a different direction, cleaning out the old limbic system filing cabinet, developing the foundation of positive thinking, and spirituality by getting us out of self and into others. In steps 7 – 9, we are systematically taught to be compassionate, think of others before we act, and take action toward change, which

triggers that third part of our brain, and drags us into spiritual activity before we even realize it.

There is a beautiful, progressive body-mind-spirit change that occurs with working 12 steps. That change takes us from a primitive brain – concerned with physical sensations, to a thinking brain that becomes progressively more able to plan, to a higher-order thought process that becomes concerned with creating peace, connecting in a positive way, and reaching out to serve others in a meaningful way that will continue to grow after step 9. So the steps actually re-educate our brain one layer at a time, just as it originally developed one layer at a time from birth to today. That re-education impacts on the body, mind and spirit – restoring balance.

Watch how we change, step by step:
1. My life is a mess, out of control. I am in pain. I am lost. HELP ME!
2. I got into this mess through my own actions, but it's all I know. If I reach out, help is there. I can be taught a better way.
3. I am yours. I'm ready. SHOW ME!
4. I have done things that aren't too "pretty." I can't deny it any more. I don't know how yet, but I know I do have to change.
5. I not only expose those "bad" things to myself, I tell someone else all about my self-loathing, how "evil" I think I am, and the "bad" things I have done. And after hearing it all, they still care about me! They say: "keep coming back." *I am not alone.*
6. Now that I have identified the "problems," I make the choice to change. I created my old life. I can create a new one. I want to stop being a ghost.
7. Now that I have identified these things, and decided that I no longer want them as part of me, I ask for the guidance to actually make lasting changes.

8. Seeing only my own needs for so long has isolated me and kept me in painful situations. If I make a list of who I have hurt, and how I contributed to their pain, I begin to see different ways to behave. I can learn to be considerate, compassionate, loving and gentle.
9. To change I have to go outside of my old self, reach out to others, use courage, faith and hope. What better way to do that than to become humble enough to say to the people I have hurt: "I'm sorry. I was wrong. How can I make it better?"
10. It really isn't all about me.
11. If I want to be at peace, I have to work hard at it, but it's worth it. I'm worth it!
12. Doing for others is an honor, and the reason I'm on the planet.

Happiness and love is our spiritual nature, and our birthright, as is the purity and innocence we first experienced at birth – before we identified with a body, school, friends, charge cards, work, pain, loss, anger and resentment. Our will is our way of doing things – what we want, what we value, and how we act according to those values. When we find ourselves in an unhappy state, we have come to the intersection of our old life and a path toward spirit that veers off into new adventure, new ways of thinking, relating, loving and receiving. All along, our own spirit was dragging us kicking and screaming toward the land of serenity, compassion, love, and acceptance. We just didn't see it that way. When we hurt we only see the pain, not the gifts of love, learning and growth in the situation. To see and appreciate the gifts that pain brings, we have to use our Neo-cortex. The last three of the 12 steps work to bring us rewards from reaching out to others, using our compassion to give, and triggering our use of our Neo-cortex by finding and holding onto spirit.

When the 12 steps speak about not "projecting" – worrying about the future, and not living in the past; they are triggering our brain in much the same way that meditation works: when we become quiet, and stop all of that frantic searching, an amazing paradox happens – we can feel what it is like to live in spirit, in the present: no worries, no pain. When we stop seeking we find. Having a tangible sense of spirit gives us a place to go back to, a way to celebrate our gratitude, and the source of creating peace in our lives – on purpose.

The lone wolf now feels his value as a member of the pack.

THE JOURNEY AND HUMAN NATURE
The meditations that follow on these pages are offered to supplement the action and changes that each of the 12 steps brings to us, one step at a time. It is suggested that you use the meditations for each step as you work that step, and then move on. The meditations are designed to match up with the mindset, needs and work of the steps and you may find that they make more sense if you allow them to unfold in a progressive fashion.

It is human nature to want to skip around and perhaps do a 12th step meditation, when in your life you have not yet finished with step one. That's not a bad thing. Meditation teachers will tell you that the important thing is doing it. Not where, when, or how well. Simply do for the sake of doing, and everything gets done. But before you start skipping around, consider this:
- If you are in early recovery or a chaotic state of mind, the meditations that are provided from step 1 through 4 are helping you to focus, to clear your head of chaos, to build a sense of competence and success inside.
- In middle recovery, or an analytical state of mind, we look at the impact of our behavior. The meditations from step 4 through 8 focus on rehearsing amends, looking at difficult parts of self, and facing difficult situations with courage and calmness.

- As recovery and serenity becomes a lifestyle, we are in a more spiritual place, already at peace to a great extent, so the final meditations are more introspective and rely less on teaching fundamentals.

If you begin your meditations with those at the end of this book you may be confused, or have trouble following. Remember our talk about the brain stem having no reason, no language? At step one your brain stem is still in charge. In middle recovery there are still so many pieces of information racing through your head that you may not be able to sit still enough to tap into calm and spirituality. If that happens, just back up, start at the beginning, practice patience, and then skip around again later to satisfy your need to have it all now.

WHAT IS MEDITATION?

The easiest definition of meditation is: focusing the mind on something, and gently returning the mind back to that thing when it wanders. The secret is that minds wander. The purpose of a mind is to think. Learning to allow that process to happen without worrying about it, then returning to focus takes practice. Remember the biggest key to success in meditating – described below:

PERSONAL ATTITUDE IS THE SECRET TO SUCCESS
Your mind is a filing cabinet where you keep all of the things that you see and experience every day of your life. That confusing mess of strange thoughts and fears running through your head is probably no weirder than anyone else's. When we get annoyed about our racing mind during meditation, our thoughts are controlling us. When we can allow our mind to wander, we have controlled our thoughts. That sounds counter-intuitive, I know. Consider this: I can become frustrated by distracting sounds or activity around me as I meditate. It is my attitude (frustration)

that will destroy my focus. The sounds will be there whether I am frustrated or not. My thoughts will be there whether I am frustrated or not, so I might as well practice acceptance, tolerance, patience, put on a smile, and begin to stop fighting and controlling. Fighting and controlling brought stress and unhappiness. Now it is time to surrender and try something else. As you practice and come to understand how you hold onto your thoughts, and acknowledge that they are only thoughts, it will become easier to let them go. We will learn how to simply put a label on all of that stuff that runs through our brain. We will learn to name it: "Just thoughts." Once we can do that, everything we worried about becomes small and no longer important.

WHY IS MEDITATION SO HARD?
Our dissatisfaction or unhappiness has nothing to do with what goes on in the outside world. It has everything to do with what we think about what happens, and how we feel inside. A lot of the difficulty in learning to meditate is about attitude and control: our desire to not let go of the things that are familiar, our desire to complicate the process, our desire to impose our will, being afraid of something that we cannot understand or change. Meditation seems hard because it forces us to look at self and grow. Change and growth are good. Change and growth are also very hard because we are required to work as hard at it as we work on our stress. We have to shift our priorities.

There are many different types of meditations. For beginners, it is a good idea to select one type and try it several times. If it doesn't seem to be a good fit with your personality, or lifestyle, try another. Some of the most common forms of meditation are:
Progressive relaxation: this is really a foundation for relaxation that has to do with relaxing muscle groups systematically, so you will see this technique a lot in the pages that follow. It focuses

our attention on our body – something tangible that we feel and understand, so it's a great place to start.

Prayer and Religious Meditation: This is most commonly the reading of religious text out loud or saying prayers within a faith. An old yoga saying about the difference between religious prayer and meditation is: "Prayer is the asking; meditation is listening for the answer."

Mantra Meditation: repeating a word or phrase over and over in the mind as a distraction for racing thoughts. Frequently, positive affirmations are used to increase compassion, decrease anger: "I will dwell on positive thoughts." You will see a bit of this style within these pages as well. This style is good for highly stressed people who cannot calm down their heads.

Transcendental Meditation™: involves allowing the mind to be aware, but not necessarily involved. Practitioners are given a mantra by their teacher. As the brain focuses on a mantra sound, and seated practice continues for about 20 minutes a day, the mind finds Bliss. Good for those easily distracted.

Tai Chi: is a martial art with over 150 different styles. It is frequently called 'moving meditation.' In Tai Chi we strive to create a blank mind, being present in the moment, present in the movements we make, concentrating on the energy circulating. Not as easy to learn as it looks, because it requires muscle memory which takes time and repetition to develop: sometimes highly stressed people want a quicker fix. Don't rule it out – it's beautiful once you allow it to grow inside of you instead of trying to force it.

Breathing Meditations: using the breath to focus thoughts. Deep relaxation breathing helps to slow down the body processes, thereby increasing the feelings of being relaxed. We will be using breathing to enhance our relaxations in the following pages.

Zen Meditation: Zen is really an overall lifestyle, but the meditations typically fall into seated styles, on a pillow, with a focus on breathing to quiet the mind; and the use of Koans: riddles or puzzles to occupy a busy mind. "What is the sound of

one hand clapping?" is a well-known Zen Koan. Chanting may also be found in Zen practice.
Chi Kung or Qigong: is a Chinese system of breathing, movement and imaging. It is used as a medicinal healing and meditative practice.

There are many, many other types and styles of meditation that you can explore. A quick search on the Internet will show you the wide variety of meditation available, and if something sparks your interest, another search of the local 'Y,' or adult classes, yoga studios, etc., will uncover great opportunities to learn. And... the most important thing for you to know about meditation before we move on:

Mindfulness Meditation: Becoming mindful means being present only in the moment and enjoying all the sensations and experiences of that moment. It sounds simple to be present in now, but it really is a much more abstract and difficult concept to grasp than it seems. Mindfulness is really the overarching goal of all forms of meditation (and 12 step work!) Becoming mindful brings us out of the past and future and into NOW, living it to the fullest, doing good work. Mindfulness is really what we all seek for a serene life.

I learned most of what I know about being mindful and living in NOW from watching dogs. Dogs are such joyful, spirited creatures simply because they only have NOW. We can walk out the door, and return seconds later, and they will joyously celebrate our return. They live in joy, and give so openly because they know only the innocence and compassion of each moment: that's one reason we like them so much – we want to share their free spirit, return to that free spiritedness of our babyhood. To really understand mindfulness, consider my dog, Cisco rummaging through the garbage for last night's leftovers while I am out of the house:

Past: If Cisco were thinking in the past, he would be worried about breaking the important house rules called: "don't eat the garbage," "no touch," and "that isn't yours."

Future: If Cisco were thinking in the future, he would be worried that I am expected home at any moment, and will be very unhappy with him when I walk in the kitchen, see garbage all over the floor, and Cisco lying in the middle of the trash gnawing on an old pork chop bone.

NOW: The only thing important to Cisco is being surrounded by wonderful stinky garbage, and the magnificent pork chop bone prize that he now experiences with every joyful cell of his body. A dog happily raiding the garbage can is the perfect definition of what it means to be mindful. It is also the perfect illustration of the state of being that meditation creates in a life. If you practice it.

WE'LL EXPLORE GUIDED IMAGERY

The style of meditation we will use in this book is primarily guided imagery. In guided imagery someone talks to you about a scene that takes you to a state of deep relaxation. Deep relaxation means that your mind and body are peaceful and serene, and the mind and body are connected to spirit, with all three of those states operating in a fluid, give-and-take. That implies that to do these images, you'll need to take one or more of the following actions:

- Read them all first and really get the content so you can do it in your head,
- Read the images into a recording device in advance - perhaps with background music - so that you can relax and listen,
- Connect with other like-minded people and take turns reading while the rest of you relax,
- Best of all: find someone with a soothing voice to read the images, record them, and everyone lay back and enjoy!

The reasons the guided imagery style of meditation was chosen for use here with teachings from the 12 steps are:
- This type of meditation is great for beginners or advanced meditators, or those of us who simply have an active mind that we have difficulty shutting down. Typically these meditations are on tape or cd, and we listen to a voice guiding us through scenery and tasks. The auditory component serves as a distraction to the mind that may be resisting relaxation: it drowns out the noise in your head. This forces you to focus, and really does the meditation for you.
- Starting a meditation group is a wonderful way to get together with other stressed out, or recovering people, and is also a wonderful way to work steps, as, creating an environment where you can all enjoy serenity is spiritual work. You can even pass the hat and collect spare change to take to the store and by new background music, essential oils, or some chamomile or green tea to share.   Meditation groups are also great for stressful workplaces. A gathering of people in a conference room for 15 minutes to a half hour can do wonders for staff morale and wellness.
- Guided images can be very versatile, and are designed to turn chaos into calm, and to help us to practice different ways of thinking and looking at situations. We learn from them.
- Guided imagery can generally be tolerated for longer time frames than other types of meditation, so you will be in a relaxed state for longer periods of time, even as a beginner. Every extra second spent in serenity is a good thing!
- Guided imagery bypasses the brain and speaks to the spirit. You don't have to believe in it for it to work. You don't always have to stay awake for it to work. Spirit always hears. Spirit is always awake.
- Guided images are the opposite of an addiction in their process and progression: the more you practice guided

imagery, the faster it works, the less you need, and the more you benefit from it. It changes life for the better.

HELPFUL INFORMATION
For some of the meditations in this book you will be asked to use a pencil and paper to make notes, or do an exercise before starting the meditation. Please do not do the exercises electronically. This is vital! The act of holding, writing, creating, having your energy on the paper is far, far superior to typing on a keyboard or dictating. Meditation is ancient. Allow your body, mind and spirit to become involved in old fashioned, ancient practices. Just because we can obtain things in a Nano-second does not mean we understand the concept of living in now. Most of our stress today comes from the fact that we are so readily accessible, everything is immediate, and everything is unnatural and digital. Turn off the cell phone, put down the laptop and pad, and allow yourself to be completely unavailable and unencumbered by technology as you explore serenity.

Stressed people can fall asleep amazingly fast. Meditation is different than sleeping, but guided imagery works even though you might doze off - because you can still hear it. Practice acceptance until your brain understands and figures out this new behavior. All of it is normal, all of it is the right way to do it, and it's all part of the process. After you've practiced a few sessions of meditation, your brain will get the idea that meditation is not nap time, and will allow your body to stay awake.

About 10% of humans can't visualize, or think in pictures. If you are one of them, (first, consider how special that makes you!), think of images as remembering something, or "knowing" about something. If the image script says: "imagine walking through a field of flowers…"don't sweat the picture – you don't have to actually see it to benefit. Remember grass, flowers as you know them – your brain will come up with something. The important thing is to breathe, relax, listen, and learn.

The 12 steps are full of information about how to be spiritual. There is no right way to work the steps: it is as individual as each person in recovery. The fact that you are using tools for the steps makes it the right way to work your recovery, and develop spiritual principles. There is no right way to be spiritual. There are techniques to follow that can give us structure as we incorporate meditation into a lifestyle. The only way you can mess up spiritual practice is to procrastinate and not do it. Tools only work when you use them.

Have you ever spaced out (while sober!) and wondered where your brain went for a few seconds? That is your brain taking a tiny vacation without your permission because it was stressed and needed a break. Through meditation, we give our brain permission to space out and find a place of peace; so the goal of mediation is to learn how to enter a controlled state of spacing out. Eventually you will find that you can stick with a meditation exercise, and actually remember it all – and even better, trigger a meditative state whenever you want, for a few seconds to hours. That is how serenity begins to infiltrate all areas of our life.

Experiencing emotion is common with guided imagery, and is a sign that it's working. Don't be afraid if emotions bubble up when you try to meditate. Don't run from it. Emotions are energy. Sadness, anger and fear may be unpleasant, but feelings are simply a sign that you are releasing energy that you've stored up inside for a very long time. In the thousands of years that people have been meditating, it has not yet killed anyone.

As you relax, you may suddenly find a need to twitch, squirm, have an anxiety attack, cough, yawn, or some other behavior. This is all normal for someone who is learning to let go. Don't worry, don't judge. The more importance you give something, the more power it has. Allow yourself the freedom to want to hold on, smile at how hard you work to be stressed. Feel compassion for yourself. This too shall pass.

Scripts are offered here on these pages. We all walk a different path. Not all of the images here will appeal to the taste of everyone. Imagery should fit with your values, comfort level and belief system. You will find images that describe sounds, smell, and visuals. The sense of smell is one of the strongest memory imprints we have. If the smell of roses reminds you of something unpleasant, change it to something you do like the smell of. If the word "God" comes up and you prefer something else, substitute your words. To recover, and learn to live a relaxed, quality life in today's' fast paced society, we will need every ounce of flexibility and creativity we can muster – use your unique qualities and thoughts to modify the scripts provided to make them more meaningful to your recovery language, your taste and your needs.

If you have other living beings in the household (room- mate, spouse, children, pets) it is a good idea to either isolate them or yourself, especially in the beginning. Explain to the humans that you need quiet time alone to practice your meditation. Close the pets on the other side of the door if they are disruptive. If you can't find sanctuary in the house, go somewhere else.

> NOTE:
> One thing you will discover about pets is that they are drawn to humans who are in a meditative state. Animals are Zen masters of mindfulness already – they loll around with their tongues out, stretching in the sun, and enjoying soft places. They like calm energy. Pets also become very interested in new behaviors and mood changes in their humans. All of us have to become used to new things, and new experiences. Pets don't speak human. We can't tell them about this new activity with

words. If you want to share this experience with your pets, by all means try it. Sit beside, or behind your pet, and focus on stroking their fur as you practice slow, deep abdominal breathing. Use the petting activity to be mindful: no thoughts, no wondering, and no dialogue. Discover the feeling of fur, see the whorls, textures and colors; the ridges of bone and muscle. Learn to simply be quiet and calm together, then teach them how to quietly snuggle, as you use the guided images in the book. BUT – give your pet a few sessions to be annoying and attention seeking as they attempt to figure out this new activity, then a couple more sessions to incorporate their understanding of their wonderful new role in your self-improvement process.

CAN MEDITATION HELP WITH CRAVINGS OR OTHER PROBLEMS?

No matter where you begin this journey, please make your first stop the heading that immediately follows this section: "PROGRESSIVE RELAXATION: DO THIS NOW AND EVERY DAY!" Progressive Relaxation is a foundation technique for relaxation that is useful, quick and easy; no matter how frazzled or serene your mind may be. If you practice this every day it will have a big impact on your overall stress in a very short period of time.

Cravings can be triggered by stress, as can "stinkin thinkin," and a host of other behaviors, attitudes and issues, because early recovery is an especially stressful and difficult situation. Meditation has a profound impact on stress levels, adrenaline levels, and negative thought processes. Regular practice will provide relief for those things, and will help you to calm yourself faster when things like cravings come up, instead of being anxious and compounding the stress and the cravings. Meditation is not a cure for anything, meaning it isn't a magic pill that will make the bad things go away overnight. The teachings and skills of the 12 steps, and the relief we get from meetings helps over time. Meditation helps over time. Put the two together and you get a boost; an acceleration of the process, which will give you additional hope, and concrete proof that life can be better.

The journey of life, recovery and hope is one we have each day that we breathe. We choose our journey, and the souvenirs we collect along the way. Breathe deep, and collect joy, serenity and compassion with a vengeance. Smile generously. Spread peace with every cell in your body. Act always out of love, unconditionally, and your abundant souvenirs will be ones that you can proudly display, and everyone will want to share.

PROGRESSIVE RELAXATION: DO THIS NOW AND EVERY DAY!

The following technique is a great stress buster, will help you to fall asleep, and is a basic foundation for triggering relaxation before many of the meditations in this book. Learn it, use it: you'll love it! The script below is one version of progressive relaxation; variations for entering a relaxed state will be repeated throughout this manual to give you an even broader range of tools.

You should close your eyes to do this meditation, but read through it first to understand the process. Breathe in through your nose and out through your mouth. To maximize the effect lie down flat on your back, arms at your sides, palms up toward the ceiling, feet about shoulder width apart.

After you lie down and close your eyes, simply remember that you're starting at the bottom, moving toward the top, breathing for relaxation. As thoughts enter your mind, smile, and bless your brain for doing such a great job at thinking. Label them "just thoughts," and go back to relaxation. There is no right or wrong way to do this. DOING it is the issue!

We Begin:

Lay back, closing your eyes. Throughout, try to remember to take deep, slow breaths and imagine that with each exhale you let go and release any tension that you may have in your body. Give each section of the body about 10 seconds before moving up to the next. Count if you want. If you feel very tense, repeat one section of the body a few times before moving on.

Focus on your feet; relax any tension in your feet.
Relax your calves. Allow your lower legs to relax, muscles becoming loose and soft. Take in a full deep breath. Release all of the tension in your lower legs as you exhale.
Relax your thighs and hamstrings. Take in a deep breath. Release the tension in your upper legs. Allow your hips to let go of any tension or tightness.
Take in a long deep breath: fill up your belly, your ribs, all the way to your shoulders. Breathe in until it hurts, hold it for a second, and let it go.
Lower back and buttocks relax. Belly soft.
Chest muscles relaxing. Muscles between your shoulder blades relax, becoming smooth and soft. Take in a full deep breath, and let it go.
Imagine your shoulders and neck muscles becoming soft, releasing all tension, all tightness, all holding.
Take in a long deep breath: fill up your belly, your ribs, all the way to your shoulders. Breathe in until it hurts, hold it for a second and let it go.
No more tension, no more tightness, no more holding.
Allow your scalp and forehead to relax, becoming soft and smooth. The muscles of your face relax. Jaw relaxes, frown lines becoming smooth.

Take in a long deep breath: fill up your belly, your ribs, all the way to your shoulders. Breathe in until it hurts, hold it for a second and let it go.
When thoughts begin wandering around in your head, bless them and let them pass.
Just watch your belly move in and out as you breathe – soft and natural.

As thoughts enter your mind, allow them to come and go.

Today is now the past and you have released all the stress of the day. Rest and float in relaxation and peace.

HUNGRY NO MORE

CREATING PEACE ON PURPOSE

A man told his grandson:

"My child, a terrible fight is going on inside of me all the time — a fight between two wolves. One is evil and represents hate, anger, control, arrogance, intolerance and superiority. The other is good, and represents joy, peace, love, understanding, humility, kindness, generosity and compassion. This same fight is going on inside you, and inside of every person in the world."

The grandson's eyes widened. His voice trembled in fear as he asked:
"Grandpa, which wolf will win?"

The old man simply replied:
"The one that you feed."

-Anonymous

Step 1: My wires are so crossed; it's time to call a repair man.

We admitted that we were powerless over our addiction, that our lives had become unmanageable.

No matter how we got that way, it is hard to admit that our lives are out of control. We want to feel grounded, and powerful. When we are working at Step 1 we are in a time of chaos: raw, stressed, fragile, out of control. We still feel close to old life, old ways, but we are tired enough that we are ready to discover something new. We are beginning a journey where we will sometimes feel very alone and vulnerable. We need to begin to calm our racing thoughts and quiet our self talk.

As we work this step we are told that life is much easier when we stop trying to control everything. We realize that the way in which we have been doing things in the past doesn't work. The purpose of this step is not to judge our self, but to enter a frame of mind that will allow honest admission and realization of what our life has become. Paradoxically, even though we enter this step feeling powerless, once we really admit our powerlessness to ourselves, we become empowered: to begin our journey toward serenity and recovery.

The promise of this step is: We are going to know a new freedom and a new happiness.
The lessons this step teaches to us are about honesty and acceptance. To incorporate honesty into our lives, we must first stop hiding from the truth, and accept things about our self and our situation. Part of that honesty is seeing how we played a part in creating our own misery. Because we are human, we make mistakes, we have limitations. Now is the time to stop hiding from our self and swallow our pride if we want to change.

The behaviors and attitudes this step helps to resolve are related to control issues, denial, grandiosity/inflated ego, scattered thought process, cravings, urges, choices, and anxiety.

You may not even know how stressed you are, or what relaxation feels like. As we begin to use meditation as part of recovery, we may find our racing thoughts intruding on the process. We may feel chaotic and frazzled energy inside of our hearts, minds and bodies. If you find yourself saying: "I can't meditate I can't turn off my thoughts…" immediately say to yourself: "I am powerless over my racing thoughts and my mind has become unmanageable…"

WHAT YOU NEED
This meditation will use a candle to assist in focus. Candles are a good beginner's meditation tool, and one that "old timers" never tire of. Go to a store that sells candles, and ask for one that drips. Most candles are dripless, meaning that the wax does not run down the sides. Don't hunt around, unless you really want to, because candles that drip are not generally obvious. Asking brings fast and less frustrating results (or shop for them on line.) The candles we seek are manufactured deliberately to run wax as a decoration, and are most often "tapers." They are typically white, but the ones we want change color to blue, yellow and red tones as the wax melts and runs, so don't be alarmed if your white candle suddenly starts dripping wax in color. The ones that run colored wax are a bit more interesting, but if unavailable, simply get any candle that drips. Try to avoid scented candles.

Now that you are ready to use your candle, be sure that the holder you use has a saucer shape, or that it is sitting on something that will catch the wax as it runs so that it doesn't damage anything it comes into contact with, or create a hazard. You will be using it on a table during meditation.

MEDITATION FOR REDUCING CHAOS: CANDLE WATCHING

Most meditation schools use candle meditations to quiet chaotic minds, to teach the concept that every day distractions don't have to take over our lives, to train the brain to focus and concentrate. Hindu meditation calls this practice "Tratak," and claim that it results in the ability to connect with Divinity and see our past, present and future without fear, but with understanding. These are all things that we will need at this stage of working the 12 steps.

HOW IT WORKS

There is something soothing and comforting about a candle flame. For some this meditation is easy, as there is a "thing" to look at and concentrate on, and that thing has a life of its own, and it is beautiful. It is normal for your eyes to wander and your brain to try to entertain itself. Allow that to happen. Don't judge, beat yourself up or become emotional about the process. Choose a grounding word like 'peace,' 'love,' 'serenity,' or something that pleases you. We will repeat this word in our heads as we begin the relaxation part of the meditation, and at any time we discover that our creative and busy brain is off thinking about something else, or worrying.

Position your candle slightly below eye level, in a spot where you don't have to hunch to look at it. You will see that we start with a variation of the progressive relaxation that was presented previously, but as you will see, it's slightly different. The idea in this variation is to tighten each muscle group, then let it go totally limp – one extreme to another. Be careful especially as you tighten your shoulders, neck and toes because those areas cramp up easily. If you do get a cramp, gently stretch the muscle in the opposite direction of the contraction and massage gently, and then begin the process from the beginning, being a little more restrained in your approach. All the while you perform the progressive relaxation, watch the flame, and enjoy how it dances.

As you stare at the candle, your peripheral vision may fade and the area around the center of your vision may become dark. You may see a color at the edges of your vision. This is normal, and is what we are aiming for. It happens due to a combination of the light of the flame, and your eyes not moving as they normally do. Allow your awareness to fade until you see nothing but the flame.

We begin:

Remember the grounding word we talked about using? Pick something now that pleases you. Use it any time your brain is off thinking about something else, or worrying.

Read through this section before trying it so that you have an understanding of what to do.

Settle into a comfortable position, but try to sit up relatively straight rather than slouched on your tail bone – we want your lungs open and accessible and your spine aligned.

Light your candle and position yourself and the candle for comfort and safety. As you go through the meditation below, simply watch the flame...

Take a nice, long deep breath and say out loud: "I've made a mess of things, I'm asking for Your help." Say your grounding word out loud.

Turn your attention to your feet. Tighten all the muscles in your feet and toes. Hold it for as long as you can. Let it go. Feel relaxation as your muscles unwind. Take in a long, deep breath, hold it, and exhale.

Tighten all the muscles in your lower legs and feet. Hold it for as long as you can. Take a long deep breath, tighten your muscles even more, hold it, and let it go. Let your ankles relax.
Take a deep breath, exhale fully. And another. Feel your muscles beginning to unwind.

Tighten all of the muscles in your thighs, buttocks and lower legs. Stretch your legs out from your body. Hold all of the lower body muscles until they shake. Take in a long deep breath: fill up your belly, your ribs, all the way to your shoulders. Breathe in until it hurts, hold it for a second, and let it go. Let go of all of the tension in your legs. Let your lower body go completely limp.

Continue watching the flame. Turn your attention to your hands and your forearms. Tighten your hands into fists; tighten the muscles in your forearms and biceps. Hold it as long as you can. Make your muscles shake. Stretch your arms out from your body. Take in a long deep breath: fill up your belly, your ribs, all the way to your shoulders. Breathe in until it hurts, hold it, and let it go. Feel warm relaxation as your muscles unwind. Take a soft, deep breath, and exhale. And again, take in all the air you can hold. Let it go.

Tighten your arms and shoulder blades and back – all of the muscles in your upper body. Hold it as long as you can. Stretch your arms out. Tighten, tighten, tighten. Take a deep breath, hold it, and then exhale, letting all of your muscles relax at once, and go limp.

Tighten your neck and throat, your eyes, eyebrows, forehead, your entire face – scrunch up your face as hard as you can. Squeeze your eyes shut as tightly as you can. Hold it as long as you can. Take in a long deep breath: fill up your belly, your ribs, all the way to your shoulders. Breathe in until it hurts, hold it for a second, and let it go. Feel the muscles in your face now smooth and soft.

Tighten every muscle in your body – stretch out your arms and legs, make a tight fist, scrunch up your face – everything tight and tense – muscles shaking. Hold it, don't let go. Take in a long deep breath: fill up your belly, your ribs, all the way to your shoulders. Breathe in until it hurts, hold it for a second, and completely let go. Feel your entire body relaxing. Muscles are now warm and loose.

Return to watching the flame. Take a deep natural breath, and say out loud: "I've made a mess of things, please help me be open to receive the caring that surrounds me." Say your grounding word out loud.

Stare at the flame as long as you can without blinking. Your eyes may water. If they do, allow the tears to come, and run down your face – just as the wax melts and runs down the side of the candle. Watch the flame; see the wax beginning to melt. Just practice calm, quiet, peace. Watching the flame...

If you find thoughts coming in, say your grounding word out loud. Concentrate on breathing and relax your belly and your muscles. If you find a tense area, tighten that muscle group; take in a long deep breath: fill up your belly, your ribs, all the way to your shoulders. Breathe in until it hurts; hold it for a second and let all of those muscles go. If you find a need to wiggle your shoulders or neck around to help you relax, go ahead.

When you think you can stare at the candle no longer without blinking, close your eyes. You should see what is called a negative after-image of the flame. Hold on to your sight of the after-image as long as you can. It will begin to fade, and it may shift and move. When it disappears, open your eyes, and stare at the flame again as long as you can without blinking. Again close your eyes and watch as the after-image recedes. Repeat as often as you want.

Whenever your mind tries to sidetrack you by thinking, use your grounding word and go back to soft, deep breathing, and gently concentrating on the flame and the melting wax again. As the wax begins to trickle down the side of the candle, imagine that one of your worries is melting and running with the wax. You may even want to say something out loud, like: "my stress is draining away," "my need to control is melting." After each drip runs down to pool at the base of the candle, take a soft, deep breath, relax your belly, and say your grounding word out loud. Continue to sit with the candle and allow your troubles to melt into the wax for as long as you wish. When you think that you are ready to stop, once more close your eyes and hold the after-image of the candle until it is gone. As you wait for the image to fade repeat the serenity prayer:

"God, grant me the serenity to accept the things I cannot change,
the courage to change the things I can, and the wisdom to know the difference."

Blow out the candle, settle into a comfortable spot with your eyes closed and just allow yourself a few minutes of quiet time. If thoughts intrude, take a deep, soft breath, bless those thoughts, and say your grounding word out loud as you exhale.

If you would like to sleep a bit, this is a good time for a nap!

Step 2: I have trouble with commitments…

> Came to believe that a Power greater than ourselves could restore us to sanity.

In step 1 we realized that we are vulnerable human beings, struggling to survive, confused – beaten by something so much more powerful than us: our life was out of control and unmanageable. When we are working at Step 2 we understand and decide that it's now time to call in outside assistance. We need something other than our own ego to sort things out. We have examples all around us of people succeeding in recovery and serenity – living examples of spirituality, hope and faith that we can use as encouragement and role models.

Step 2 brings us the knowledge that in recovery we can use a source of strength outside of our self to find a better life. We discover that wisdom and protection is available from people around us, and sometimes from forces we can't see. Before serenity can take hold, we must have faith, and believe that we are connected to healing and a Higher Power. We don't have to be religious. We do have to come to terms with the concept that we aren't alone; we can be connected to others safely, and there is a goodness; an energy in the environment of recovery that surrounds us. Many people call that energy a power greater than self. We can use that energy for support:

- For some, that power greater than self is called "God."
- For some it is the energy and power of the rooms and the group: a support system of people.
- It may be nature, love, life force, or internal strength and courage.

The promise of this step is: We will not regret the past nor wish to shut the door on it.

The lessons that this step teaches us are related to respect, reaching out, and developing hope and faith in self, others, and a power greater than all of us.

The behaviors and attitudes we begin to resolve in step 2 are related to acceptance, doubt, isolation, fear, trusting others, and belief in our own strength. To develop serenity we have to believe that serenity is possible. Before a Higher Power can take over we have to have faith. Change and growth requires determination, action, and the stubborn pursuit of hope.

WHAT YOU NEED
A pencil, notebook.
A tree, preferably in a wooded area, or park so that you have the space and freedom to be quiet, comfortable, and alone.

Some people just don't feel comfortable or safe outside in early recovery. That's normal. If you feel more comfortable indoors, or if you don't live in an area where trees are readily accessible; or weather does not permit outdoor activity, locate a picture of a beautiful tree to keep the image alive. Continue with the directed meditation as if you were outside. Allow your imagination to fill in and act as if you were with a tree outdoors.

EXERCISE:
Before actually doing the meditation, sit down with pencil and paper and make a list of all of the things that you would like to get rid of from your old (or present) life.
Put the list in your pocket, along with a pencil, grab a bottle of water, and head for the outdoors if you are able to be outside.

MEDITATION FOR LETTING GO AND GROUNDING: TREE TALK

Tree talk is a very old Hindu meditation technique. From ancient times and through many cultures there have been great symbolism surrounding trees. From trees we get medicines: Willow bark gives us aspirin, Yew trees are used in cancer medications, Dogwood can help with malaria. Oak trees, throughout almost all cultures are revered for their size and long life. We hear fables and tales of enchanted woods, of spirits and magical creatures living in trees. Spend some time with a tree, and you will experience nature as healing and grounding. We tend to see trees as solid, strong, powerful, fresh, and full of energy and life. It is good to use grounding each day, so every chance you get, go out and be in nature, and incorporate nature into your search for serenity.

If you are able to get outdoors to a park, your yard, or a trail in the woods, we will begin this meditation by politely introducing our self to a tree. If you are practicing indoors, begin by studying your picture of a tree. If you can, use a woodsy scent like cedar essential oil to enhance the experience (see the back of this book for additional information about use of essential oils.) Then introduce yourself to the tree as if you were there with it in nature: follow along as a guided visualization.

This all may sound like a silly thing to do, but it's an old Hindu tradition: whenever we engage with other forms of life we should practice courtesy, honor, dignity and grace, and those other forms of life will show us honor in return. Accept and respect this ritual that is thousands of years old! It will make you smile as it unfolds – roll with it!

We begin:

As you wander along, pick out a tree that appeals to you in some way. Stand quietly for a moment, and send the tree a greeting, and a request to join you in meditation. You may say this out loud, whisper, or form the question in your mind. If you don't get an impression that the tree agrees, move on and select another one. You may have to introduce yourself to a few trees before you find your ideal tree. (If you are indoors, you would have viewed several pictures before selecting the one that appealed to you. Continue as if the tree agrees to spend time with you.)

If you think the tree agrees, walk up to it and touch the bark lightly, introduce yourself in any way that you see fit. Tell the tree that there are many things on your mind at the moment. Thank the tree for agreeing to help you to sort out your thoughts. Allow your fingers to rest lightly on the bark and feel the texture. Compliment the tree on its color, shape, leaves – anything that comes to mind. If you feel silly speaking out loud, talk to the tree in your mind. You may feel silly any way. Don't worry about it, feeling silly is better than chaotic, powerless and unmanageable, right? Sometimes we just need to do for the sake of doing.

Leave your hands resting on the bark, and begin telling the tree your story, tell it your fears, talk about the chaos in your life, your hopes and dreams. Many people like to sit facing the tree with their palms and forehead resting on the tree as they talk. Or you may want to turn around and lean your back on the tree, allowing your hands to go behind you so you can rest your fingertips on the trunk. Feel free to tell the tree anything that comes to your mind, until you have a sense that you have gotten it all out.

When you have nothing more of your personal story to tell, allow your forehead, or one cheek to rest on the bark and ask the tree for one last favor in helping you to gain strength and feel more grounded and at peace. Take out the list you made of all of the things that you want to get rid of. Read them one at a time to the tree. As you read each one, stop for a few moments, look up toward the sky, through the branches, and listen for a rustle of leaves and branches as the air moves through them. Imagine that the tree is taking the things that hurt, and is sending them one at a time up through its' branches, toward the clouds to be carried away. Once it is gone, take your pencil and cross it off the list, then move to the next thing you have listed.

Move through your list slowly, deliberately, and with each item, listen to it being taken away in the rustle of the branches. When your list is complete, close your eyes, relax against the tree and say the Serenity Prayer. Allow yourself time to simply sit quietly and do nothing. Study the tree. Some trees are scarred by lightning, insects or man. Consider those scars, and the impact the injury and pain may have had on that giant, vibrant form of life. Think about the effort the tree may have had to use to overcome drought, injury, cold and hardships as it grew. Imagine what stories that tree must have, standing there for so long – who has spoken to it this way? What has it shared, given to all of us? Enjoy your surroundings, close your eyes… the important thing is to remain there and simply exist for a while. Let some quiet and gratitude creep in.

Now we come to the most important part of the meditation: Tell your tree how grateful you are for the chance to share its time and energy; to have the tree hear your story, and take away your secrets and worries. Feel gratitude wrap around you. Smile. Rest a little while longer with the tree and absorb the quiet and calm that is all around you in nature. Breathe deeply. Use all of your senses: ears to hear the sounds of life around you, fingers to feel texture of the tree, nose to smell the scents around you, your eyes to see bark, branches, leaves, sky. Use your heart to connect with the solid strength of your tree and imagine sending your gratitude into the tree and down through the roots, connecting with the spirit of nature.

Thank the tree and wish it well, or say a prayer for the tree before you move on.

Step 3:   HELP! ...show me another way...

Made a decision to turn our will and our lives over to the care of God as we understood Him

Step 1 is about understanding that things are a mess, and we need help. Step 2 is when we believe that change is available: we have found help. You'll know you're really ready to turn things over when you begin to feel a sense of peace creeping in. Calm and peace, no matter how small, are indications that you have developed faith and hope through working the first two steps.

Step 3 is a decision – to give up the old for the unknown; but with the hope, faith and promise of a new life as we allow outside influences to help us. We can stop "Looking for Love in All the Wrong Places," and begin to enjoy connecting, exploring spirituality, and allowing a Higher Power into our life. Through this step we can let go of our fear that everything will fall apart. Stress, fear, unhappiness, anger, frustration... are all about trying to control things that we can't. That is why letting go is the real challenge in this step: we can't manipulate or control something outside of our self (God/Higher Power, nature, other people.)

The promise of this step is: We will comprehend the word 'serenity.'   To gain the promise of this step we will experiment with how to use a Higher Power as we begin to explore meaning and purpose in new ways.

The lesson this step teaches is about faith, integrity, and caring. As we look at our strengths and character defects we will be summoning up integrity to own those parts of us that may not be pleasant. There are many recovering people who are available to us, and are ready to help, and the only thing they ask of us is an open mind and willingness. To care for self, and to accept caring from others will become a spiritual principle in our recovery because it teaches us how to be a compassionate person who can willingly and happily extend a hand to someone else in need.

The behaviors and attitudes this step helps to resolve are related to identity and image of self, embarrassment, intimacy, resistance, ability to change, need for immediate gratification ("I want it NOW!"), fear of failure, anxiety.

Through step 3, we will also discover the power, and the paradox of our thought process:
The harder we look for meaning, it more it eludes us.
To have pleasure in life we have to be willing to experience pain.
To find our personal power we have to stop striving for it.
The very thing that we are trying to find seems to be visible in others, but not within our self.
When we give up control we find it, and feel spirit.
When we let go of chaos we find calm.
When we dwell on anything, it exists and looms larger – when we stop dwelling on it, it no longer exists.

WHAT YOU NEED
Again, if you aren't comfortable going outdoors to meditate, you have no trees/wooded areas, or weather doesn't permit it, select a picture that is close to the scenario described. If you can go outdoors, grab a bottle of water, and head out so that you can use nature to ground you. Bring a blanket to spread on the ground.

Look for a place where there are trees, pine needles, and the wonderful smell of pine. If you don't have such a place nearby, head for a park or a group of trees, and modify the script to meet your needs.

If you are remaining indoors for this exercise, spread a blanket on the floor in a cozy spot in your house, and relax there as if you were able to be in nature. Essential oils can also be an adjunct to meditation work if you can't be outdoors. Review the chapter in the back of this book on how to use oils. For this meditation, if you don't have pine trees at your disposal, essential oils of cedar, pine and other "woodsy" scents are readily available. Follow directions on the bottle. Most don't advocate applying to the skin. You can put a drop on your blanket, or on a tissue that you can place nearby.

The script that follows is for someone seated, but you may adapt if you'd rather lie down on your blanket.

DANCING CHILD MEDITATION
Find a soft spot to spread your blanket and sit in a comfortable position. Close your eyes, just relax and listen to the world around you, as you breathe deep for a few moments. We will use a variation of progressive relaxation:

We begin:

Sit comfortably, hands resting on your thighs. Close your eyes and begin to breathe deep into your belly – in for a slow count of 4, hold for 4, out for a count of 4.

Inhale for a slow count of 4, focus your attention on your feet and tighten all of the muscles in your feet, holding for a slow count of 4, exhale, releasing all of your muscles as you exhale. Inhale, focusing on your legs. Tighten all of your leg muscles; stretch your legs out, holding as tight as you can for a count of 4, exhale, then relax all of your muscles.
Inhale for a slow count of 4, focus on your belly and buttocks. Tighten all of your muscles, holding as tight as you can for a count of 4, exhale, then release.
Focus on your hands. Make a fist, tighten as hard as you can, inhale for a count of 4, hold for a count of 4, exhale, then let go.

Focus on your arms. Inhale for a count of 4. Make fists again, tighten all of your arm muscles and stretch your arms out from your body, hold, tightening for a count of 4, then release as you breathe out.

Tighten your face muscles as hard as you can, breathe in, hold, exhale and release.

Tighten every muscle in your body, stretch out your arms and legs, tighten even more, inhale for a count of 4, hold for a slow count of 4 and let everything go limp with your breath out.

Take a slow, deep breath in, and exhale.

Think of yourself sitting alone in the woods on soft, fragrant leaves and pine needles, with your eyes closed. Imagine a canopy of trees overhead. You are sitting quietly, listening to the sounds of nature around you, enjoying the deep scent of the forest. Take a slow, deep breath in for a slow count of 4, hold for 4, and exhale. Just pause for a bit, enjoy sitting with stillness. Nice, slow, deep natural breaths. The temperature is perfect, the air smells wonderful... birds are chirping...

You hear a small rustling sound nearby, and someone giggling. As you open your eyes, you see a small child of about 4 years old dancing around in a circle under the trees. The child is not too far away from you, but does not see you sitting quietly on your blanket. Watch as the child is dancing, giggling, so happy to simply turn in circles, and celebrating life as only a child can do. The child spins, arms stretched out, hair flying. The child becomes dizzy from dancing, and tumbles down onto the soft forest floor, giggling, rolling on the soft pine needles. Notice the flushed chubby cheeks, the soft shining hair, sparkling eyes and huge smile.

The child sits up, and begins to play in the pine needles: pushing, poking, scooping them up, throwing them into the air, mounding them into shapes. The child finds a stick and pokes around in the soft ground, searching for bugs, and treasures.

Cheeks flushed, hair tousled, happy and smiling, this beautiful child is focused on all of the wonderful things that nature and the forest has to offer.
This child looks very familiar to you…

Study what the child is wearing. Study the color of their hair, the way they move. As the sun filters through the branches, it lights up the child's hair and makes it sparkle. Something about this child pulls at your heart, tugs at your memory… Now you realize that the child looks so much like you did at that age…

You want to say something to this beautiful child, but they are so absorbed in play that you are afraid to scare them. Say a greeting in your mind - as if you could project your thoughts quietly into the child's mind. The child seems to hear your message, because they look up. A huge smile spreads over the child's face when they see you, and the child waves, as if they recognize you too. After smiling at you for a moment longer, the little child returns to playing in the pine needles.

Look down to the ground at the moss, pine needles, leaves, twigs and stones on the forest floor all around you. Begin to run your fingers through them just like the child does. Think of a gift that you would like to give to this child. Use your imagination, compassion, memories of things you wanted at that age. Don't worry about the materials not matching what you want to make, or your ability to sculpt. There is magic here, under the trees: as you pick up pine needles, nuts, stones, grass, moss – any of the tools nature has left for you, it will all transform into any color, texture, shape, or form that you want. Make something that will bring the biggest smile to the child's face.

Sit back for a moment and study the gift you have made: What did you make? What color is it? How big is it? What is the texture? Why did you choose that particular thing? Imagine that you could fill the gift that you are about to give with all of the love, hugs and tenderness this beautiful child will ever need.

You hear a giggle, and as you look up, you see that the child has been watching you as you worked. The child is amused at how serious you are, and how focused you are on your task as you finish making this special object. Hold your gift up so that the child can see it. As the child sees what you hold in your hands, you are rewarded with a huge smile. The child's eyes sparkle as they get up, and run toward you, holding their hands open. As you give the child the gift, they wrap their arms around it, hugging it close, with the most beautiful smile you have ever seen. The child dances again in circles, laughing and happy with this new toy.

As the child hugs the gift so tightly, it suddenly begins to glow with yellow, sparkling light. As you watch, your gift has turned into transparent, warm, yellow light, and seems to be dissolving into the area just below the child's heart. The child giggles, and their tiny hands cross over their ribs as the light disappears into their lower chest. Slowly the light begins to ooze from inside of their skin until the child has warm, glowing yellow light all around them.

This glowing, happy, giggling child holds out both tiny hands for you to take – hands that are so warm, so full of life, they seem to vibrate and tingle. Smile as you are rewarded with a giggle. Allow that giggle to infect you until you cannot help but join in. The child looks up into your eyes. You belong together. The beautiful yellow light that surrounds the child begins to wrap around both of you now. Feel the warmth running up through your palms, and see the glow begin to ooze through the skin on your hands and arms, working its way throughout your entire body and moving through your skin to cover you in a warm sparkling yellow glow. Feel a tingle of warmth just below your own heart. Both of you begin to turn in a circle, hands joined, moving faster and faster, allowing the giggles to take you over. As you begin to feel dizzy from spinning, kneel down and accept the hug offered by this beautiful child: wrap your arms around, holding them close, eyes closed, feeling innocent, joyful happiness creeping into your heart. Just as the toy that you made began to melt into warm, yellow light, so does the child. As you hold each other, the child becomes lighter and lighter. And as the child did with your toy, cross your hands over your chest and allow the light to melt into the area just below your heart.

Sparkling yellow light now seems to ooze from all over your skin. Sit down once again on the pine needles, close your eyes, and listen to the sounds of life around you. See yourself still glowing with warm yellow light. Smile. Search your mind for all of the warmth, happiness, and relaxation inside of you and dwell on it, make it grow.

As you sit quietly, with your eyes closed, enjoying the peace, a small rustling sound and a giggle nearby tells you that a small child still sits in the pine needles, not far away from you in the forest. You don't even have to open your eyes to look. That child is with you, in your heart.

Take a long deep breath, allow yourself to feel so light and free that you could toss pine needles into the air, giggle and dance in circles with the sunbeams shining on your hair until you fall down laughing. Feel free to do just that before you pack up to go on with your day.

Step 4 - Soul-searching, soul searing secrets

Made a searching and fearless moral inventory of ourselves, and when we were wrong, promptly admitted it.

Your favorite restaurant has an inventory process to be sure that their supplies and equipment are readily available for the dinner rush. We all have to know what we have in our internal store room, and what condition the goods are in so we can meet the needs of life. We should all take regular inventory. Self-examination will tell us what we have in the cupboards, and what we need to do for prep work.

The first 3 steps helped us to sort out our head. Step 4 helps us to find our heart, and the wounds and sadness that we hold deep inside of it. The action of Step 4 is in confronting our worst enemy: our self; as we dredge up shame, guilt, memories and feelings. But in our store room, we will also find areas we can change and rearrange to begin our new life; defining our moral and spiritual values and principles, and seeing the cause and effect between our thoughts, actions and the impact of our behavior on others. That is one of the reasons we fear this step so much: no one wants to hurt. Paradoxically, being able to hurt, cope with it, and then sort through what it means to us in a calm fashion makes it hurt less.

We are human, we make mistakes. To incorporate honesty into our lives, we will need to stop hiding from the truth. We have survived addiction. Addiction is catastrophic. There may have been kinder and gentler ways to live life than what we chose, but we did the best we could with what we had, and we faced huge obstacles that were painful, difficult and beyond the comprehension of "normal" people. Through our fourth step, as we let go of pride, sorrow, and sort through our wounds and our fears, we will find a hero inside of ourselves that has courage and worth beyond measure.

The promise of this step is: No matter how far down the scale we have gone, we will see how our experience can benefit others. *The lessons* that this step teaches are integrity and honesty. When we can face our pain honestly, head-on, and begin learning to give our self a break, our hurts loom over us less and less, and the pain begins to evolve into strength, wisdom, courage, understanding and grace.
The behaviors and attitudes this step helps to resolve are related to denial, dignity, minimization, excuses, resentment, fear, self-acceptance, arrogance, perfectionism, self-pity, loneliness, shame, guilt, remorse.

Because we are human, we don't like to confront our mistakes. Our ego wants to remain in charge and save face. These kinds of negative thinking patterns occur because we have not yet figured out that we have to forgive our self and let go. This meditation will focus on containers and boxes full of your 'baggage' that will be loaded on to onto a boat, train, bus, truck so that they can be taken away. Here are some options for outdoor environments that might fit into this meditation:
- Train tracks, preferably running through a spot where you can sit beside them undisturbed and safe.
- A place where trucks are loaded for delivery.
- A bus or train terminal where people are going away for distances.
- Loading docks of any kind.

If you choose a busy loading place, find a seat off to the side where you are on the "fringes." If you don't have anything similar to a rail, bus, truck terminal near you, or can't venture out at the present time, you can use pictures from a magazine of a freight train if you need to enhance the visuals, or simply relax and let your imagination unfold and take you to a place where the images work.

WHAT YOU NEED
A bottle of water would be good – if you're in the mood for a field trip.
A pencil and notebook.

EXERCISE:
Start by making a list of things you are still holding on to. List as many things as you'd like: control issues, anger, fear, perfectionism, people pleasing, denial, resistance... the sky is the limit, and each of the things you are holding onto will have a place in this exercise. The things that you have been holding on to can be things you have been carrying around for a lifetime, a few years, or today. You are free to let go of them now, because they are no longer useful, and somewhere, someone else will have a need for these things.

Being spontaneous also works well for this meditation, so you can do it from your head without a formal list if you'd like. It is helpful to do this type of exercise frequently because surrender is not easy! Don't worry; if you're holding onto something and you don't get to it the first time, you have many more days of living to do this meditation again, and again, and again ...

MEDITATION FOR LETTING GO: "I THINK I CAN, I THINK I CAN..."

The script that follows speaks as if we were about to load our containers onto a train. Feel free to modify this image to suit your needs. If you choose to go to an outside location for this, sit quietly off to the side, on a bench or chair and allow the activity of people to just exist all around you as you watch and play the scenario in your mind.

We begin:

Settle into a comfortable position with your list. We will be imagining that each person, situation, or thing that you want to let go of is packed into a container, box, suitcase or crate. Imagine each one of your containers to be as big and heavy as that thing is for you to carry. That may mean that you'll need to use your imagination and memory banks to conjure up forklifts, machinery, and workers to help. Some of the containers may be small enough for you to toss on board yourself. Other pieces of your baggage may be so huge they need a crane.

We will start with progressive relaxation:
Focus on your feet; relax the tension in your feet.
Relax your calves. Allow your lower legs to relax, muscles becoming loose and soft. Take in a full deep breath. Release all tension in your lower legs. Let it go.
Relax your thighs and hamstrings. Take in a full deep breath. Release the tension in your upper legs. Allow your hips to let go of any tension or tightness.
Take in a long deep breath: fill up your belly, your ribs, all the way to your shoulders. Breathe in until it hurts, hold it, and let it go.
Lower back and buttocks relax. Belly soft.
Chest muscles relax. Muscles between your shoulder blades relax: becoming smooth and soft. Take in a full deep breath and let it go.
Imagine your shoulders and neck muscles becoming soft, releasing all tension, all tightness, all holding.
Take in a long deep breath: fill up your belly, your ribs, all the way to your shoulders. Breathe in until it hurts, hold it; and let it go.
No more tension, no more tightness, no more holding.

Allow your scalp and forehead to relax, becoming soft and smooth. The muscles of your face relax. Jaw relaxes, frown lines becoming smooth.
Take in a long deep breath: fill up your belly, your ribs, all the way to your shoulders. Breathe in until it hurts, hold it for a second and let it go.
When thoughts begin wandering around in your head, bless them and let them pass.
Just watch your belly move in and out as you breathe – soft and natural.
As thoughts enter your mind, allow them to come and go.
Close your eyes for a moment just relax and listen to the sound of your own breathing.

There is a freight train waiting to be loaded with suitcases, parcels, crates. Think about all of the details of that train: does the train have a name painted on it? Where is it from? Where is it bound for? Are the cars all different colors, or the same? How long is the train? Try to imagine a conductor standing beside your train with a lantern in one hand, and a sign in the other that says: "Destination: Hungry Ghost Land."

There are piles of boxes, crates and parcels stacked near the train for loading. Workers are getting ready to begin loading the crates and baggage, and they are waiting for you to inspect and approve of each suitcase, crate, or box before they can load them for shipping. Put on a set of imaginary coveralls, and a hard hat. See yourself walk over to one worker, who hands you a marker and a clip board. Go over to a box, and as you look inside, you'll see something from your list that you want to let go of: it may be "grief," "sadness," "anger," "abusive relationships…" Take your marker, write the name of the contents on the side of the box, then give a nod to the workers who will close it, seal it tight, and stack it on the train. Listen to the sounds of packing tape being unwound, the sounds of wooden crates being nailed shut, workers calling to each other, sometimes grunting under their load...

Continue working with your inspection and your labeling of each suitcase, box, crate... Have fun trying to imagine what type of container is needed for each thing you want to get rid of, and it will appear before you, in its container, ready for inspection and shipping. How heavy is each one? Toss a few onto the pile yourself, just to feel the freedom of letting go, and the sense of helping. Are any of your boxes marked 'fragile?' If you want to continue to treat this baggage with tender loving care, carry it gently and place it on the "outgoing" pile yourself. If you are finished with this baggage, drop it, kick it, and ruin it, before putting it on the pile if you wish.

If it seems like there are too many packages, don't worry: there will be as much shipping space, as many cars on the train as you need. Keep inspecting, labeling and directing the loading process for as long as you want. If you have your list with you, check off items one by one as they are loaded for shipping.

As you look around, you'll see that the loading platform seems to be getting empty. Check your list one more time, look everywhere, under things, behind things, be sure you have gotten everything, then stand and look at all that has been loaded. Take a moment to run through your mind for anything you may want to add to the piles for shipping, and then box them up and carry the items onto the train car. Be sure it is all boxed up tightly, and stashed away safely on the train. Reach up and pull the heavy door closed, sealing the car, ready for movement. Give a signal, and at each train car, a worker will pull the heavy door shut, and call out "Ready!"

Step back onto the platform a bit and look down the length of your train. This is a lifetime of worry, character defects, anger, fear, and loss... all that you've carried around with you for so long. As you stand and take in the sight of the packed freight cars, you will hear someone yell "Last call! All aboard!" The train begins to start up. Hear the chugging of the locomotive, the movement of equipment as the forklifts and cranes move to a safe distance, off to load another train for someone else.

Take in a deep breath and watch as the train slowly begins to creep forward, away from you. You may feel a bit sad at giving up something that you have known for so long. There are many wonderful, new things out there to replace the things that are now slowly moving away. Feel a sense of relief that you no longer have to carry those things, relief that they are slowly chugging away, packed and wrapped with loving care. Your train is quite long, and it begins picking up speed. The freight cars pass you one at a time, filled with your baggage, moving faster and faster. How many freight cars did you fill? Watch the cars one by one as they pick up speed...

Take in a long, deep breath, and understand that these things were keeping you from growing and experiencing life fully, peacefully, happily. All of those packages were connections that tied you to living in the past. Some of those connected you to unhealthy situations. As the train picks up more speed, the wheels begin to rumble on the tracks. You begin to feel light and free. Watch the train go until it is so tiny it disappears on the horizon. Take in a long deep, natural breath. All of the things that you have sent away served you well during your time together. Each had a job to do for you, and did that job well. Each played a part in making you who you are today. Bring one of your packages into your mind and think of a valuable and positive lesson that you learned from the contents of that package. Think of a reason to be grateful for having that thing in your life. Bring others to mind one at a time: what did you learn from your grief? From your perfectionism? How did denial serve you well? From what or whom did your anger protect you? Bless them one by one, and feel happy that you had such wonderful tools to serve you so well when you needed them the most.

The train has disappeared over the horizon. Think of all of the reasons to be grateful for having had all of that baggage to carry; and for now having the opportunity to lighten your load. Prepare yourself to leave the loading area: take off your imaginary work clothes, give back your imaginary hard hat, marker, and clip board. Take a deep breath and stretch. Pause for a moment and think about how good it feels to have tidied up a little, to have made room in your head and heart for new people and experiences. Open your eyes.

If you went outside to a location, pick up anything you brought with you, stand up, and begin walking away from your meditation spot. Use all of your senses: see everything around you – notice nature, people moving and working, activity all around. Breathe in smells. Hear the sounds of people talking and moving through their day.

If you still feel bothered by some of the things you thought you had packed up and sent off, understand that this is normal – it takes time and practice to fully let go. Allow yourself to look around at the sky, the sun, trees, or even clouds and rain, and have gratitude. Think about nature, recovery, possibilities, and Higher Power; and how soothing it is to be in a place of beginning to let go and move toward healing. Moving toward means that we aren't there yet, but we can get a glimpse...

By now your train is long gone, and you may have trouble remembering what you put in some of those boxes. That means healing has begun. Smile.

Step 5: Confessions

Admitted to God, to ourselves and to another human being the exact nature of our wrongs

It is hard to admit that our lives are out of control. We want to feel grounded, and powerful. But in the past, we may have behaved in ways that damaged relationships and connections. We may have done things that we would rather leave in the past and never think about again.

Up to now we have been working hard on the last four steps to accept, let go, forgive, make amends – and we may be feeling a bit of relief because of our hard work. Now it is time to dredge it all back up, and share who we are with others. As we bring up things that are difficult to deal with, those memories may bring with them a lot of things like being abandoned, uncertainty, and the process of having to make amends… Don't worry, as you were working hard on those last four steps, you were also developing skills and relationships. Now it is time to practice how to use those tools.

We all mess things up; it's human to be flawed. Through this step we learn that shame is optional, but guilt is not. When we are caught in shame, we are alone and think that we are unworthy and defective. Now it is time to embrace the shame that we created in our illness and our past actions, and transform it into guilt. Guilt is thinking, or knowing that we could have acted differently. When we can take the shame and turn it into guilt we can connect to others.

Addiction is an illness of isolation. Step 5 gets us ready to see our role in damaged relationships, and helps us to understand that we did what we knew how to do at the time. Through this step we understand how our illness is so much a part of everything we do, and even who we are. We will need humility from the steps that came before this so that we have the strength to hold our head high. When we admit our wrongs out loud to another person, we also can see our 'rights,' and become humble enough to say "I'm sorry." The end result of this step is to feel lighter, renewed, and ready to move forward.

In step 5, all of the faith, trust, acceptance, hope, and understanding that we have been practicing in the beginning steps will connect us to hope, faith, Higher Power and people in the program who will stand strong beside us, and hold us up when, and if, we fall. And as we grow they will teach us about forgiveness.

The promise of this step is: No matter how far down the scale we have gone, we will see how our experience can benefit others. *The lesson* that step 5 teaches is the importance of truth. When we share with someone else, we are making room for new interpretations, new connections – so we will also learn to listen. *The behaviors and attitudes* this step helps to resolve are related to honesty, procrastination, pride, isolation, trust, forgiveness. Each part of us that we face will help us to grow stronger and our thoughts to become calmer and clearer. We learned to be the way we are now. We can learn a new way. We can use meditation to begin to develop acceptance and healing. As we reach out and begin to release the toxic thoughts, feelings and actions of the past we also begin to lose that sense of isolation. When we can confess the worst of our self to another person, we learn what it is like to really trust.

WHAT YOU NEED
Soft music, less than 60 beats per minute. Japanese flute might be a good choice, or soft chant.
Grab a bottle of water, and head for the outdoors if you can, so that you can use nature to ground you. As we've done before, if you can't get outside, use a photo to help you to imagine.

A pencil, notebook.

EXERCISE:
Before doing the meditation, sit down with pencil and paper and make a list of all of the things that you regret in your inventory, or if you used a journal for your inventory, get your journal book to refer to.

This style is called "listening" meditation. When being taught this form of meditation, students are often told that it is in the space between words, between the notes of music, that we find spirit. To tap into spirit, to connect to Higher Power, we have to become comfortable listening to silence. Because we live in a fast paced, world of digital noise, silence can be one of the hardest things to listen to.

Typically, in listening meditations, we ask a question to understand something that we want clarity on, such as: "What am I here to do?" and then we simply wait. Others, like the one we will use here, incorporate images. We will use images to create a dialogue so that you have small moments of silence to consider, and you can listen to the messages that your heart sends. Keep in mind that listening meditations take practice and can't be forced. Go with it and resist the desire to look for an answer, just let it unfold. If you have trouble listening, practice gently. Repetition results in learning and understanding.

A LISTENING MEDITATION FOR FORGIVING: CREATE A PEACEFUL HEART BY SAYING "I FORGIVE…"

Sit or lie comfortably where you will not be disturbed. If you go outdoors, sit with your back leaning against a big tree. Out of respect for all life forms, remember to stop for a minute and begin this meditation by politely introducing yourself to the tree. Stand quietly for a moment and send the tree a request to join you in meditation. If you don't get an impression that the tree agrees, move on and select another one. If you think the tree agrees, walk up to it and touch the bark lightly, introduce yourself in any way that you see fit. Thank the tree for agreeing to help you to sort out your thoughts.

We begin:

As we move through this image, we will think about asking a question. We all possess a wisdom inside of us that allows us to be calm, objective and insightful when we are listening. These meditations help to train the brain to sort through the chaos and find our inner spiritual voice.

Focus on slow, deep relaxed and natural breathing. Notice the coolness of the air as it goes in, how much your body has warmed your breath as you exhale. As you take in a long, deep, natural breath, begin counting backward from 10. Take a deep breath, again studying the change in temperature of the air: think about the number 9... 8... 7... Continue counting down through the numbers, considering each one slowly and deliberately until you get to one.

Rest for a moment and breathe, just feel the air change temperature on the inside of your nose, as it is warmed by your body.

Think of standing on a path at the edge of the woods, the sun warming your back; the coolness of the woods is in front of you. The path is soft with dense pine needles and leaves – like a carpet. Your footsteps are quiet as you walk. There is stillness all around you: a hush. The path is very wide, easy to see, easy to follow. Think of yourself walking down the path, and as you walk, listen to the sound of the breeze in the trees, birds singing. Listen to the scratchy, rustling sounds made by small animals as they move along the ground, searching for nuts and berries, chasing each other in play. As you pass, they pay you no mind, they are not afraid of you… almost as if you aren't really there…or as though you are one of them. They know that you mean them no harm.

As you wander, enjoy the variety of trees, bushes, flowers. Up ahead on the path there is a clearing in the trees. As you move closer, you see a small pool of clear water bubbling up from the ground: a natural spring. The sun sparkles on the bubbling waters, and beautiful, red dragon flies buzz throughout the area. Flowers splash color all around. There are broad, flat rocks all around the edge of the spring, and as you touch one you see that they are warm from the sun. Choose one to sit on. There are beautiful, brightly colored fish in the pond, and they rise to the surface, looking back at you. A dragon fly begins to buzz near you. As you stretch out a finger, it buzzes over to perch with you for a while, watching you with big, round eyes. Smile for the gift of being able to hold this amazing creature.

Close your eyes and just exist: sitting comfortably on the warm rock, with your eyes closed, enjoying the warm sun, the deep, rich smells, and the quiet sounds of the woods. Very close to you is a sound so soft that you aren't sure that you even heard it. As you open your eyes, you will see that see a person – who appears to be ancient and very wise – has sat down next to you on a rock, and is also enjoying the serenity of the woods. That wise person is there to teach and speak with you, support you, and help you to understand how to face things, how to grow, how to forgive. Study their face for a moment: the wrinkles around the eyes, study their skin, their hair, their clothes, their quiet, peaceful manner: eyes closed, face turned up to the sky, relaxed and smiling. The old one makes eye contact with you, and says softly: "We have all done things in the past that we regret. This is a good place to learn about forgiveness; a good place to heal." They ask you to talk about a hurtful situation from your past.

Choose a situation from the list that you made, a time when you have "wronged" someone, or yourself. Before you talk to your companion, replay the scene in your head from start to finish. Be calm and objective, as if you were watching a movie. If you begin to feel tense, take in a slow, deep breath, and tell your teacher that you feel nervous, that the situation has hurt you, and the pain is still there. Take in another gentle, deep breath. Your companion says: "Your past can't be changed, but your future can be different. It can only hurt you now if you allow it. Tell me the story."

Tell this wise person all of the details of what happened. Begin with: "I am having trouble forgiving myself because I am guilty of..." (Tell the story).

Pause after you speak, and allow stillness as this wise person absorbs and thinks about all that you said. Listen to your own thoughts as they arise. If you feel your shoulders getting tight, your jaw clenching, this is natural. It's all just a part of letting go. Breathe deeply and softly and consciously tell your muscles to relax. Describe to the old one what happens when you think about the situation – what is happening to you right now. Use slow, soft, deep breathing. Say: "Old Friend, whenever I think about what I did, I feel..." (ex. angry, afraid, shame, etc.)

Imagine that they rub their chin in deep thought before replying: "Has anyone you know ever done something similar? Tell me the story of what they did."

Tell the story. Your companion replies: "Should this person be tortured for making those past mistakes? Tell me what should happen to them as a result of their actions. Tell me what it might mean to them to be forgiven."

Describe what you think should happen to that person. Pause for a moment. Take in as many soft deep breaths as you need to relax. Visualize your situation again. Imagine the shame, anger, hurt, on the face of the person you wronged. Talk to your companion about the character defect that led you to act that way, and how you feel about yourself now. Tell your wise teacher whatever runs through your head about your actions, your thoughts at the time. Finish your story by saying: "It happened to me a long time ago, but it still hurts a lot, and I don't know how to let it go."

The wise one responds with: "Back then, you used the skills and the knowledge that you had. You did the best that you could with what you knew at the time – do you see that? We can't do things differently until we understand how – until we learn a new way. We sometimes do hurtful things because we care so much. Sometimes we drive others away because we can't stand to hurt them any longer, or don't want them to watch us hurting our self. We hurt those we care about. But - can you find the caring in what you did?"

Breathe deeply. Relax. Be still and look for the caring in the situation. Listen to your heart for a few moments until you have an answer to this difficult question. Tell your teacher: "Here is where I see the caring under the hurt and my actions..."

Your teacher says: "Giving to others from a loving and peaceful heart is the first step toward forgiveness."

Think about how you would ask for forgiveness from the person you hurt, allowing yourself to feel, breathing deeply and remaining relaxed. What would you say? How would you act? Play the scene in your mind with a peaceful heart.

Look for the lesson you learned in your conversation with your wise teacher, and say:

"My role in turning this around will be to ..."

Sit in stillness next to your companion. Close your eyes and just be there together. Imagine warm sun on your skin. Rest quietly for a moment and think about all the wonderful people and things that are now in your life. Review how you feel, turn over the lessons you have learned, the gratitude that you have for all of those wonderful people. Smile and enjoy a warm, peaceful sensation all over. Focus on slow, relaxed breathing – no effort. Sit and relax for as long as you want the meditation to continue.

It's time to go. Imagine standing, and thanking your companion for being there to listen to you. Tell the wise one all of the things that you are grateful for. Your teacher smiles, bows their head and turns to walk away silently through the trees.

Breathe deeply and softly. This is the first step toward forgiving yourself.

When you are ready, take a full deep breath, wiggle around a little to work out any kinks, stretch like a cat: enjoy all of your muscles. When you are ready, open your eyes.

Step 6: I can't hide any more...

Were entirely ready to have God remove all of these defects of character

"The mind is everything. What you think you become."   - Buddha

As we approach step 6, we have owned our past and have accepted that it's over and we can't change it. This helps us to understand our own behaviors, motivations and how to impose self consequences for the future. By now, we have given up trying to control everyone and everything. We have taken a long hard look at our self, our behavior and the consequences of our actions. We have swallowed our pride and made amends. We can now start walking a path that will give us the positive life that we want, with strong relationships that are built in trust and compassion. In coming as far as step 6, we are beginning to learn how to weave our 'bad' qualities – our defects of character – together with our 'good' qualities to make a new person (actually the person we have been all along, but with less denial and resistance.)

Buddha also says: "As we examine our defects of character, we will see how our faulty, negative thinking helped to keep us in the land of hungry ghosts." As we practice the steps, our meditations, form positive relationships, and use all of the tools available to us, our thoughts begin to change and our mind connects to more positive people, places, things and Higher Power. Those positive connections that our mind makes will ultimately shape our world. As we grow into our new view of our self and our world, we may find that the spirituality we have developed is changing our inner language as well. That is the big tip off that it's working because you simply worked it! For instance, at step one; we may have said something like:

"God, please take these bad feelings away from me, PLEASE!"
Now our inner language has changed, and we might say it more like:
"I am afraid. I know that You, the program, other people and my own strength and hard work will get me through it. It works if I work it. Thank You for being there!"

The promise of this step is: That feeling of uselessness and self-pity will disappear.
The lesson that this step teaches is willingness. In step three we practiced surrendering. Step six helps us to see that surrender is a way of life, and we learn how to surrender in a much different way: we will give up the parts of our self that we uncovered in our inventory, and discover something amazing in that void that we never knew existed. Think of it this way: in our meditation of loading boxes on a train, we emptied things no longer useful, and watched as our old, unwanted baggage was carried off. To do that, we needed to be willing to really let it go. It's a fair bet that afterward we all tripped over some of that old baggage that we thought we sent away in that meditation, because we weren't really done with it yet. Having things happen in stages, and having to repeat things to learn is all part of the process. Like ghosts, our old ways come back to hang around and haunt us. In this step, we don't just send away the old stuff, we fill the empty space with positive feelings and thoughts, that way there will not be enough room to reacquire and recycle the old. And we won't miss it. This is where the construction of our new being comes in. The things we will begin to hoard in this step are joyful, light as a feather, and take up as much room as a spring breeze – so plan on hoarding a lot of it!
The behaviors and attitudes step six helps to resolve are related to issues of ego, guilt, old patterns of behavior, willfulness, security, confidence, self-image and self-esteem. Step six is cleaning out the cob webs and making room for positive actions, and living life with love and positive attitude.

WHAT YOU NEED
Quiet room, soft lights, and warm temperature, soft, soothing music, pleasing and relaxing scents.

MEDITATION FOR COMING TO TERMS: HEALING THE BEAST

Just as we created the negative parts of self, we can create new, positive parts:

"It takes a lot of work to cultivate ugly. It takes a lot of work to cultivate beauty. Which would you rather have growing on your farmland, Missy?"

-Mom

This meditation will help us to further separate our past actions, judgments, and memories from who we really are. This type of meditation can be the road toward healing, because it helps us to draw that line between self and past. Our goal in this meditation is to look right at the ugly that we may still see inside of us, and watch it disappear. We may believe that since we created such a negative part of our self that we *are* that negative part. Not true. Humans are many things. Being inherently negative is not one of them. It happens by choice.

We begin:

It is common as we do this type of meditation to bring memories to the present. Remember: no harm has come to anyone from meditation. The past can't hurt you unless you let it. You are completely in charge of how nervous, angry, fearful or happy you want to be.

Lay back, closing your eyes. Take deep, slow breaths and imagine with each exhale you let go of any tension, tightness and holding: focus your attention on each part of your body, stop in each area, and take a couple of full, deep breaths:

Focus on your feet; relax any tension in your feet as you breathe out slowly and softly.

Relax your calves as you breathe out. Allow your lower legs to relax, becoming more comfortable and at ease.

Relax your thighs and hamstrings. Allow your hips to let go of tension. Allow your entire lower body to let go. Lower back and buttocks relax. Belly soft.

Ribs let go of tension.

Chest muscles and the muscles between your shoulder blades relax becoming smooth and soft.

Imagine your shoulders and neck muscles becoming soft, releasing all tension and tightness. No more holding.

Take a deep breath and just let go.

Relax your shoulders into your upper arms, elbows, forearms, wrists, and hands.

Allow your scalp and forehead to relax, becoming soft and smooth.

Take a deep breath and allow the muscles of your to face relax. Feel your eyelids heavy and relaxed, no tension around the eyes, no squinting.

Take a few deep, slow breaths and really enjoy releasing tension.

Today is becoming the past, whatever has happened is over. Let it go. When thoughts wander into your mind, take a deep breath, bless them and imagine blowing them into the room as you exhale.

Just watch your belly move in and out as you breathe – soft and natural. Watch your ribcage expand and contract. Every exhale removes more stress and tension.

Bring one of your character defects to mind (yes, only one!) It can be one that has been troubling you a lot, one that you think is gone or resolved, or one that you are beginning to successfully reduce. We are going to play an imagination game where we turn your character defect into a monster, a dragon, a beast of your imagining – have fun with creating it in detail.

Think of the character defect that you would like to let go of, and imagine what it might look like if it were standing in front of you as that beast or a monster. For example, if you want to get rid of a hostile, angry attitude, you might think of it as a huge fire breathing dragon that scares everyone away, or a scowling troll with a huge wooden club.

Manufacture your monster in your mind in detail. Answer these questions thoroughly, one at a time, trying to actually picture it all before moving on:
What color is it?
How big is it?
Does it have fangs?
     Wings?
          Talons?
               Scales?
What does it smell like?
     Is it slimy?
          What is it doing?
How does it act toward other people?
What does it sound like?
What job does it have?
When your monster is in charge, what happens around you?
Do you call it to come out and work for you, or does it turn up all by itself?
Why do you want it to go away?
Give it a name. Tell it: "Your name is…."

Now think of yourself as sitting in a big comfortable chair, in a beautiful room, surrounded by books, with a fireplace, large windows that let in the sun. Look around you in this beautiful room and feel comfortable – like you never want to leave.

Through the windows you can see a beautiful garden full of blooming flowers and trees. Sun beams come through the window and fall over the rich, soft carpets, soft light wraps around you, relaxing you even more. The fire crackles in the fireplace. Your chair is so soft and comfortable that you never want to get up. Wrap the serenity and warmth around you and smile.

Your monster stands in front of you, shifting from one foot to another, looking as if it wants to fight. It grumbles, and seems prickly. It is anxious to take over your life at a moment's notice. Don't allow its impatience to get inside of you. Just let it shift back and forth, restless. Take a soft, deep breath; work on letting go of any tension as you study your monster without emotion. Sink back into your comfy chair, close your eyes, feeling lazy and content, feeling the warm sunlight coming through the window. Feel the sunlight as healing, rejuvenating, melting away any stress or tension. Don't worry about your creature; it can wait while you enjoy the warmth. The monster – your "defect" – will stand quietly, shifting from one foot to another, wringing its hands, waiting for you to pay attention to it. Just watch your belly move in and out as you breathe softly and naturally. Every exhale removing more stress and tension.

Imagine that the sun beams are slowly turning from yellow to a beautiful, cool, sparkling, deep emerald green. Imagine that green light is also streaming down all over your "defect" as it stands, looming over you, and waiting. The sparkling, green light also begins to have a calming effect on your monster: the beast slowly stops its restless behavior, and stands quietly, watching you. Feel the energy inside of you and in the whole room as relaxed and comfortable. You didn't get involved in fighting with your "defect," you have created an atmosphere of calm, serenity.

In active addiction, in stress, in strong emotional states, in desperate times, we sometimes act from the dark places of our self to survive. Sometimes when we look at negative parts of our self, or our actions, we feel guilt or shame, because we know we didn't act out of a place of caring and compassion, or didn't see the love in the situation. Those actions are the past. What we did is over. Now you can make new choices. You can't fix the ones that you have already acted on. We have to let those actions exist in the past.

The character defect standing in front of you has come from your own imagination. You conjured it up and gave it life as a terrible monster. Take a slow, deep, natural breath, open your eyes and look at the monster you created again. Say its name, and tell it which defect of character it represents.
Say its name again, and tell it softly and gently:
"I needed you once, but I don't need you anymore."

Don't feel bad, or worry about the creature. Close your eyes again. Think about the three parts of you:
1. Your body sits in the chair, in a beautiful, peaceful place, trying to relax.
2. Your mind has conjured up the monster that lived in your heart for a very long time. Your mind judges your actions and who you are, as if the past were happening NOW. If you listen to your mind, and allow yourself to be stuck in the past, the monster will always be with you, as a weight in your heart.
3. If you feel guilt, sadness, anger, remorse, and shame – if you want things to be different – you are hearing the voice of your own spirit. Your spirit is telling you the way toward growth.

Open your eyes and see that huge, nasty, dark, ugly beast; waiting for your attention. It is still surrounded by that soothing, healing emerald green light. You creature is now quieter than you have ever known it to be. Funny... is it smaller...?

It now answers you by saying: "I know. I understand." Take a full, deep, natural breath, and imagine that with each exhale that the monster begins to shrink. Imagine that the sparkling green light grows brighter around the beast as it gets smaller and smaller; until it is just a tiny little thing standing in the light, shielding its eyes from the brightness. A helpless, lost little creature. It squeaks. It has become so small that it can now fit in your hand.

Say its name and tell it gently and softly: "You have been with me for so long – through it all, but I made the choice to change. Our work together is over."

It nods its head and answers: "I know. I understand."

Take a deep, slow breath, bend down and hold out your hands. Allow your creature to scramble into your hands, where it squeaks softly, turns in a circle, and curls up in the safety and comfort of your warm palms. Feel gratitude for how this once huge, dark, horrible beast served you so well, protected you so well. For years it was all that you had. It got you through the rough parts, it took the pain, and it fought long and hard with sharp teeth and claws.

The tiny thing yawns, and curls up, snuggling into your warm hands; now vulnerable. Now you are protecting it. Let it settle in as you lean back into your comfy chair. You are all that keeps it here now. As you cradle the tiny thing in your hands, close your eyes, and feel lightness in your heart and mind. It sleeps now in the cradle of your palms, on your lap. Allow gratitude to grow inside of you for having the relationship with this noble, wonderful beast for so long.

You slowly begin to feel as light as a feather. Imagine yourself so light that you float upward through the roof, toward the clouds. Enjoy the sensation of floating. Enjoy the relaxation as you float among the clouds – over rooftops and trees... Breathe deep and naturally. There are only soft clouds, and you, holding your tiny creature gently in your hands as it rests – so small and light in your palm, snoring softly. The poor little thing is exhausted. There is no need to feel bad that it used to be huge, that it was so strong - that you took its power away. Feel compassion for this tired creature: it has worked so hard. It deserves rest and peace. No need for guilt.

Call the creature gently by its name, and tell it how thankful you are for your time together, how grateful you are for all that it has done to help you. You may want to tell it the story of a time when it fought so bravely to protect you when you felt vulnerable and scared. Thank it for being so brave and for taking on your pain. Take a finger and stroke it gently.

Say its name again, and tell it: "It's time for us to say goodbye. You can rest after working so hard for me for so long. You will need your rest so you can build up your strength for the next person who needs you."

Imagine a tear of happiness running down the tiny cheek and dropping onto your palm. It squeaks happily, thanks you in a quiet little voice, and reaches out to you as if to give you a hug. Smile, close your eyes, pet the beast softly, and enjoy the time you have to say good bye and be at peace with each other, as you float with the clouds.

Suddenly, you notice: your creature has disappeared.

Place your hands over your heart and feel the warmth of your palms. Remember your creature again with a smile. You have both been released.

Take a soft, deep breath, wiggle your fingers and toes, stretch long, and really enjoy the stretch – like a sleepy cat. Allow yourself to feel light and peaceful as you continue your day.

Step 7: I'm standing here naked

Humbly asked God to remove our shortcomings.

When we begin working a 7th step, we may find uncomfortable feelings of powerlessness returning because we are looking closely at our self, and focusing on our faults. When we focus on the negative parts of self, we trigger negative self talk. Negative self talk puts us in brain stem reactionary mode, and our stress can increase. People who are stressed typically have a mindset that they are powerless to change the situation they are in, and have trouble seeing a way out. That is also typical of early sobriety. It is a normal part of the process: what we focus on grows. If we focus on our shortcomings, we will see only our shortcomings. When it's temporary, and for a purpose, that isn't a bad thing, because when we look at our shortcomings objectively and honestly, we develop humility. Humility gives us a new perspective. That new perspective will transform our negative self talk into new attitudes.

The seventh step is the beginning of the final purging. That's why we may feel as if we're suddenly back at step 1: in the final hour of anything, we all tend to have an adrenaline surge, go for broke, and hang on for dear life to what we know best. It's okay – hang on with greasy fingers, and when you finally slip into the void, embrace change with open arms and a smile!

Worrying about being worried is counterproductive.

The promise of this step is: We will lose interest in selfish things and gain interest in our fellows.
The lesson that this step teaches is humility: this step takes the concepts from the previous six and turns them into action – we begin to get to know our sense of spirituality by having a frank, open discussion about our self. To be frank and open we have

to get down, dirty and honest. It's a humbling, and strengthening experience.

The behaviors and attitudes this step helps to resolve are related to honesty and integrity. We find power other than our own ego. That power will help us to grow from the spirit. In step 7 we begin to develop character, incorporate honesty into our lives, stop hiding the truth, and accept things about our self and our situation.

WHAT YOU NEED
A pencil, notebook.

EXERCISE:
Before doing the meditation, sit down with pencil and paper and make a list of your shortcomings – the things about you that you would like to change.

AFFIRMING MEDITATION: SERENITY IN THE EYE OF THE STORM

Because in step 7, we are again looking at difficult things, and dredging up the past, emotions can run high. High emotional states can scatter the thoughts and create chaos where there was calm. As we begin to use meditation during step 7 work, we may find racing thoughts intruding again, and frazzled energy inside of our hearts, minds and bodies, just as we did way back during our first step work. If you find yourself saying "I can't meditate I can't turn off my racing thoughts anymore... what's wrong with me?" go back to what we learned in the first meditation, and immediately say to yourself: "I am powerless over my racing thoughts and my mind has become unmanageable." Smile and carry on with the task. It's okay.

We begin:

Make yourself comfortable, feet flat on the floor hands on your thighs, eyes closed.
Allow yourself to relax. No need to fight negative thoughts in your racing mind – the chaos in your head will come and go. Let your brain do what it needs to.

Inhale. Relax your scalp and head. Imagine that there are three tiny tornadoes in your body, running around in your head, cleaning out the cobwebs and chaos. As you breathe out, imagine blowing those little tornadoes into the room, where they disappear.
Relax your face and ears. Send the little tornadoes around inside of your head and exhale tension and stress along with them into the room.
Inhale deeply, sending the tornadoes to clean through your neck, shoulders and throat. As you exhale, let all the muscles of your neck and shoulders relax.
Breathe in, sending two little tornadoes down through both arms, to sweep out the stress in your arms and hands. Exhale them out into the room. Feel the relaxation setting in.
Inhale. As you send tornadoes down through your body to sweep up stress, your chest and upper back relaxes. Exhale the stress into the room.
Inhale, sending several little tornadoes swirling all through your body, through your back and stomach. Blow them out into the room as you breathe out.
Take in a soft, deep breath, feel the tension leaving your body as you exhale.
You can feel your thighs relaxing as you send tornadoes to clear out the tightness. Let the muscles completely go as you breathe out.
Take another breath, sending tornadoes all the way down to your feet. Let your legs go limp as you exhale them into the room.

As you breathe in, send one more batch of tornadoes running around inside of you to scoop up any left-over tension and tightness. Allow all of your tension to dissolve as you exhale.

Think of a huge hurricane, swirling in a circular pattern, as you've seen them on a weather map: a big, swirling mass of clouds. Breathe deeply and naturally. Think about news reports of hurricanes, and the chaos from the wind, the blinding rain, the darkness that swirls around on the ground.
Breathe in deeply and softly out.

Think of the parts of your life that are like a hurricane. Where in your life are those big, swirling masses of clouds? Breathe deeply, and naturally, as you focus on the confusing, messy, stormy areas of your life, the things that are chaotic, and your shortcomings. Concentrate on one of those shortcomings. Follow the thought with a slow deep breath. Say to yourself: "I am not perfect. I'm human. I have flaws. It's okay. Being flawed is what being human is all about." Allow all of your tensions to go as you exhale.

As you review your shortcoming, you may discover other things in your life or relationships that aren't going your way. See how you are continuing to allow the negative energy in your mind to fuel the storm until it becomes completely furious and out of control. Follow each of those thoughts with a slow deep breath. Say to yourself: "I am not perfect. I'm human. I have flaws. Everyone has flaws. Being flawed is what being human is all about."

Imagine that you are seated in a lake, in a small wooden rowboat, rowing out toward the center. There are beautiful reflections of trees on the water. The day is a comfortable temperature, but there are clouds, and it feels as though a storm is coming. Even though it isn't bright, sunny and a perfect day, you are enjoying the lake, nature, and the opportunity to be alone with your thoughts and spirit. Just be at peace as you row across the water, watching fish jump in the distance. The sky is quickly becoming dark, but you continue on toward the center of the lake.

The huge storm moves in so fast... the wind picks up, whipping your hair. Birds are flying for shelter in the trees. Huge raindrops are beginning to fall. The water is becoming choppy with waves, the boat rocks; water begins splashing over the edge of the boat. All around you the wind is whipping, rain is stinging your skin. On the seat next to you are a compass, a big book of directions, and an anchor at your feet. As you see those items, tell yourself: "I am safe. I am capable. I have everything I need with me. I have faith that I can get through this storm."

The storm is furious, and you must hold on to the sides, you can row no more. It seems dangerous, as if you might be completely swamped... but somehow you are not afraid. You aren't cold. You are staying in your seat. It's almost as if you sit in your own little protective bubble. Tell yourself: "I am safe. I am calm. I have faith that I can do this. A Higher Power surrounds me, and will get me through this storm."

All you can do is sit in the boat on the rough water and wait it out. Breathe slowly, deeply and naturally. You can be calm in chaos. Picture a hurricane from the weather map in your mind. Hurricanes have an eye: a calm center. As a hurricane travels, the eye of the storm provides a lull to regroup. You are sitting in the chaos of storm now, but the eye of that storm is approaching. The furious hurricane is moving past you. Think of the storm slowly moving past you until the wind, the noise, the rain slows down and the warmth of the sun comes out. Allow yourself to feel the warmth, and wrap it around you as you continue slow, deep natural breaths. The sky above you is now a bright blue. It is sunny, no clouds, the perfect temperature. The chaos of the storm continues to move onward, but you are now wrapped in calm energy at its center. Life around you may be out of control, but you sit apart from it, quiet and calm. You could move forward, backward – in any direction, and jump back into the storm if you'd like; but you sit quietly, safe and serene in the center of chaos; unaffected. Tell yourself: "Everything may frantic and stressful, but I don't have to be part of it. I can be calm in chaos."

Slow your breathing down until you feel yourself more and more relaxed. Enjoy the quiet. Tell yourself: "Good things happen to me every day and I am surrounded by good people."
Take a deep breath and repeat to yourself: "Good things happen to me every day and I am surrounded by good people." Think of them one by one. Remember the gifts you receive from them each day.

Imagine picking up the big book of directions next to you, flip through the pages, and allow your finger to stop at random. You read: "Believing that we are being cared for is a result of developing a relationship with a Power greater than ourselves."

Follow that thought with another slow deep breath and an affirmation: "I am safe. I am calm and capable. I have caring people around me. I am at peace. I have so much to be grateful for."

Feel the wind of the storm pick up a bit as the storm continues to travel on. The calm center is giving way to chaotic winds again. Think about another of your shortcomings. Follow this thought with a slow deep breath. Say an affirmation to yourself: "I have caring people around me. I am at peace. I have so much to be grateful for." List in your mind all of the blessings that you now have, all of the things you have learned that have made your life easier, better, richer. Feel gratitude.

The wind is howling again as the storm moves on its journey. Tell yourself: "If I want a Higher Power to remove my shortcomings, I have to get out of the way and allow it to happen."

The storm becomes as furious as before. All you can do is hang on and sit, waiting for it to pass once again. Ask for your shortcomings, sadness, your issues, to be lifted from your shoulders, and imagine that as the storm passes over you, and picks up momentum, it is lifting up all of your issues and shortcomings one at a time, and they swirl upward to join with the chaos of the wind and rain. See your shortcomings explode into sparks as the lightning strikes them. Allow the chaos to exist all around you but breathe deeply, knowing that the storm is using your internal chaos as fuel, to continue traveling faster on its journey. Feel more and more tension leaving your body as you exhale, and the hurricane winds carry your stress away.

The storm is now almost over. The wind, the noise, and the rain slow down and the warmth of the sun comes out again. It is over. Imagine the sky above you, bright blue, sunny, no clouds. Stress, worry, has all been washed away and the world smells clean and fresh, as it does after a cleansing storm. Say an affirmation to yourself: "I am able to change. My life can be calm. I can create joy for myself and the wonderful people around me. Stress and negativity are a temporary storm."

Say a prayer of gratitude. Wiggle your fingers and toes, stretch like a cat in the sun, and enjoy the feeling of stretching muscles.

The man whispered, "God speak to me."
And a meadowlark sang. But the man did not hear.
So the man yelled, "**God, speak to me!**"
Thunder rolled across the sky. But the man did not listen.
The man looked around and said, "God, let me see you."
A star shone brightly. But he noticed it not.
And the man shouted, "**God, show me a miracle!**"
And a life was born. But the man was unaware.
So, the man cried out in despair, *"**Touch me, God, and let me know that you are here!**"*
God reached down and touched the man.
But the man brushed the butterfly away, and walked on.

-Anonymous.

Step 8: Willing to love unconditionally in a land of extremes

Made a list of all persons we had harmed, and became willing to make amends to them all

Never underestimate the impact of thinking ahead and planning when you have difficult tasks to complete. In our 8th step we make a list, but this is not just an innocent paper full of names, this is a list of all of those people that we have hurt. As we begin our list, we will again be reviewing our past, our mistakes: as each person comes to mind so will the pain, damage and guilt and shame. As we become ready to start this amends process, all Hell breaks loose, and we find ourselves surrounded once again by extremes. This is a normal reaction to stress, and gives us a great opportunity to practice all of our skills for patience, calmness and cultivation of positive attitudes.

We need to learn how to solve life's problems in new ways. This step is where we begin cleaning up the past, undoing, making peace as best we can with our self and others. The overall goal of the steps is to teach us to be a better person. The people on our step 8 list become our pathway to becoming more compassionate, living a life of spirituality and service, giving instead of taking. Our amends to them are the pathway to freedom and peace: for all of us.

We may never really know how many people we hurt with our self-centered actions. Almost all of the pain from the past has another person connected to it: family, friends, even strangers. During addiction, we sometimes live by rules similar to these:
- I don't care that I hurt you, leave you hungry, lie to you, cheat on you, and steal from you.

- I wouldn't be using if I cared about myself, and since I don't care about me, I can't care about you.
- I don't care what I have to do to meet my needs, and I will do things that are extreme.
- I will hurt you again and again and again …as much as I am hurting myself.

Your list of damages may be quite long. When you see those names in black and white, you may become overwhelmed. At a time like this, you need other people in your life in a healthy way. You have many of them in the program, willing to help. If you feel overwhelmed as you begin this step, reach out, open your mouth and take care of your needs. The first person we should all put on our list for making amends is our self.

>NOTE:
>
>This may sound strange, but think about including your pets in your list of amends! Meditation and eastern philosophy teach us that all life forms are sacred, and there is spirituality in our relationships with all forms of life. In your addiction, did you care for them well? Do your character defects sometimes result in you being impatient, irritable or inconsiderate to your pets? When your stress is not in check, do you overlook their needs? Our relationship with our pets is a spiritual relationship that needs nurturing and care as well.

The promise of this step is: Self-seeking will slip away.
The lesson that this step teaches is love: our reason for being on the planet is to serve others, and a Higher Power. Service is the highest form of spirituality. Service is unconditional love and acceptance.
The behaviors and attitudes this step helps to resolve are related to humility, control issues, denial, grandiosity/inflated ego,

scattered thought process, urges, choices, willingness, surrender and anxiety.

WHAT YOU NEED
Soft music, low lights.
Essential oils can enhance this meditation, but follow the directions for use, as some are not recommended for application directly to the skin. Incense and sprays are also good choices. Some suggestions follow of scents that come from the forest or create a woodsy atmosphere:
Cedarwood - calming, comforting, strengthening
Myrrh - spirituality, balance
Cypress -mental power
Pine – strengthening
Ylang Ylang – balances energies, peace and confidence.

MEDITATION: FIRE AND ICE

Meditation cleans out the cobwebs in the brain, and the spirit. Meditation can teach us a method of creating warmth, softness, and compassion no matter where we are, or what is going on around us. Use your brain, and some creativity, and the stress management techniques you have been practicing so far to help you to find some balance.

We begin:

Get comfortable, lie back, and close your eyes.
Focus on your feet; relax the tension in your feet.
Relax your calves. Allow your lower legs to relax, muscles becoming loose and soft. Take in a full deep breath. Release all tension in your lower legs. Let it go.
Relax your thighs and hamstrings. Take in a full deep breath. Release the tension in your upper legs. Allow your hips to let go of any tension or tightness.

Take in a long deep breath: fill up your belly, your ribs, all the way to your shoulders. Breathe in until it hurts, hold it, and let it go.
Lower back and buttocks relax. Belly soft.
Chest muscles relax. Muscles between your shoulder blades relax: becoming smooth and soft. Take in a full deep breath and let it go.
Imagine your shoulders and neck muscles becoming soft, releasing all tension, all tightness, all holding. Take in a long deep breath: fill up your belly, your ribs, all the way to your shoulders. Breathe in until it hurts, hold it; and let it go.
Allow your scalp and forehead to relax, becoming soft and smooth. The muscles of your face relax. Jaw relaxes, frown lines becoming smooth.
Take in a long deep breath: fill up your belly, your ribs, all the way to your shoulders. Breathe in until it hurts, hold it for a second and let it go.
When thoughts begin wandering around in your head, bless them and let them pass.
Just watch your belly move in and out as you breathe – soft and natural.
As thoughts enter your mind, allow them to come and go.
Close your eyes; just relax and listen to the sound of your own breathing.

Think of yourself as standing in a mountain meadow. See the incline of the mountains as they rise upward. The meadow is surrounded by a pine forest. It is a bright, crisp night, with a full moon, and fresh sparkling virgin snow all over the ground. Huge snowflakes fall. Although the air is crisp and cold, cold enough to bring out the blush in your cheeks, you are wrapped in a coat that is soft, feather light and soothingly warm, your hood is up. Your light gloves and boots are warm and comfortable for walking. You feel energized by the sharp cold air, and the snow. Your steps are light and easy as you begin walking up the slope toward the tree line. The moon is so bright you can see for miles. Stop walking and close your eyes for a moment, and feel the cool air coming into your nostrils as you breathe, and enjoy the contrast as your body warms the air with each exhale. Listen to the hush all around you - the quiet that comes with a snow fall. Wrap the peace around you: as soft and light and warm as your coat.

Ahead is a path in the woods. Continue to walk toward the break in the trees, listen to the crunch of your footsteps on the frozen ground, the soft whisper of the snowflakes falling softly all around you. Ahead on the snow you can see the sparkles of flakes, like diamonds, beautiful, clean, reflecting the moonlight. Feel your heart rate rise a bit as you walk, your breath becoming deeper, muscles becoming warm from the walking. Watch the steam of your breath in the cold air. Stick out your tongue and catch a few snowflakes, enjoying the feeling as they immediately melt on contact with the heat of your body. To one side, deer are grazing in the meadow, nuzzling the snow aside for blades of grass. They look up as you walk past them, curious, but not afraid. The moon hangs huge, full and heavy over the trees.

You are surrounded by tall, ancient pines with huge trunks. They are heavy with pine cones. As you go through the opening in the trees, the snow underfoot gives way to soft fragrant pine needles. Your footsteps are soft on the pine needles, and the scent of pine rises up with each step. The snow makes a soft sound as it settles on the branches. The air is clean and deeply fragrant; the smell of moss, old wood, pine, and damp earth is all around you. This forest is ancient, full of powerful energy, full of wisdom and grace, and its energy wraps around you, making you a part of it. The old pines talk to you in the movement of their branches. Soft snow whispers as it falls, animals are moving around you. Among the pines are more deer, wandering and grazing, so close you could touch them as you walk by. Feel gratitude for being able to be so close to such beautiful wild creatures. The scent of pine is everywhere. The moon is so bright that you can see to walk without difficulty. Enjoy the lightness of your steps and the beauty of the night as you continue to walk up the slope, through the trees.

Through the trees ahead you see a soft orange and red glow. As you walk toward it, you find a flat, circular clearing in the trees. In the center of that clearing are large flat rocks in a huge ring, and within that circle of stones are burning logs, stacked in a pyramid – a bonfire. As you stand at the edge of the clearing you can feel the coolness of the forest behind you, and the warmth of the fire on your face. The logs hiss and crackle. Overhead the night sky is clear and the moon is heavy and low. There are huge, brilliant stars. Sparks drift upward and disappear in the stars.

As you walk toward the fire, lower your hood, remove your gloves, and enjoy the glowing warmth on your skin. Feel that warmth melting away any tension that you may have. Imagine that you can pull pieces of paper from your pocket, each one already crumbled into a ball. Each paper has something written on it: something that still troubles you about the past. You don't have to see the paper to know what each one says. Hold the little balls of paper one by one in your hand, and say out loud what is written on each, something like: "I have been angry. Thank you anger for helping me to:_____, but I don't need to be angry anymore."

Toss the paper ball into the fire. As you toss in the ball of paper, sparks rise high and crackle on the air, drifting upward toward the stars. Toss your papers one by one into the fire, reciting and blessing each one until you run out. Pause to watch the sparks from each paper ball as they burn, crackling and rising up. Your sparks are now joining with the stars, and they multiply. The stars are so big and bright it seems as if you could touch them. Enjoy the fire, the warmth, and the feelings of serenity. Look up to study the stars: you'll see the Milky Way, the Big Dipper, and the North Star. Some of those stars have been made from your troubles as you let them go. You are now surrounded by more stars than you have ever imagined.

Take a deep breath, close your eyes and enjoy the warmth of the fire on your face, the sweet smell of the burning wood. Look up once more at the sparkling stars, so bright, so joyful, and so beautiful. Walk around the perimeter of the fire pit, enjoying the scent of the wood, the crisp night air, the beauty all around you. As you come back to the path in the tree line, turn around slowly and feel the cold, crisp night air of the forest on your cheeks. Pull on your gloves, your hood, and begin walking back through the snow to the forest path. Listen to the crunch of your footsteps on the frozen ground, the soft whisper of the snowflakes falling softly all around you.

You enter the woods, and again the snow gives way to pine needles, leaves and twigs. As you pass the deer on your way homeward, smile as you approach. What can you give them? Remove your gloves, stand still, and hold your hands out, palms up in offering. The deer approach you, nuzzle your pockets, nibble at your hood, and lick the moisture of the huge snowflakes from your fingertips. Smile as they investigate you with curiosity, nudge you gently with affection. They seem grateful for your offering. They wiggle their ears, flick their tails and wander on, quietly grazing through the forest, comfortable to have shared your peace.

As you continue homeward, think about everything that you can to give to others. Think of the wonderful qualities that are you. Plan some small things that you can do to serve others today.

Enjoy a stretch, a cup of tea or glass of water, and know that you can carry this lightness with you through the rest of your day. Know that you shine as brightly as the moon, the stars.

Understand that serenity, and compassion are gifts that you can give to others.

Step 9: "Ya gotta have courage."
-Cowardly Lion

Made direct amends to such people wherever possible, except when to do so would injure them or others

As we enter step 9, we may feel small as we begin restitution: facing those with whom we have created conflict. The thought of sitting with another person to confess in step 5 was frightening enough, now we will approach people we have likely been avoiding because of strong emotion around the past that we share. Step 9 challenges us to stand strong and look inside of our self for the causes of our actions, accept what we have done, and find the strength to try to undo the pain we caused to our self and others: through action, not just talk. As we make amends, we turn our denial inside-out and we discover that all of those things that happened to us are not on the outside, like "people, places and things," those things are locked in our hearts. There is a paradox in this step: we may feel powerless, but as we take action, we discover that we have been very powerful all along. We had choices all along.

It is never easy to face someone we have hurt and summon up the courage to ask "what can I do to make it right?" Working this step doesn't depend on others allowing us to make restitution, this step forces us to see our own hope, courage, strength, faith, and all of the other positive and spiritual qualities and values we have deep inside. We are now in a position to use every positive quality we have to do the right thing. The recovery and healing is in our willingness. Making amends, acknowledging the hurt, holding your head up with grace is an amazing gift you can give to everyone involved in the situation. The most important thing about this step is the fact that no matter how the other person answers our quest, or what the outcome may be, growth happens.

It is also important at this step to look at individuals who have harmed you, and practice compassion and forgiveness toward them. Resentment, anger and negativity toward others is the kind of thinking that causes and reinforces self harm.

The promise of this step is: Our whole attitude and outlook upon life will change.
The lesson that this step teaches is courage. After the self-examination in our fourth step, and the confessions of the fifth, we now have to confront a lot of feelings and memories.
The behaviors and attitudes that step 9 resolves are denial, procrastination, responsibility and resistance, spiritual values and principles, and our sense of justice. In this step we are focused on "right" and "wrong", and restitution.

If you were a football player working through anxiety about a kicking a goal, you might imagine getting up in front of everyone, ready to kick, breathing deeply, as your anxiety about kicking between the goal posts crept in. Before actually kicking the ball, there is a need to be centered and grounded, and in a positive frame of mind. To condition your mind against apprehension about succeeding in kicking that goal, you would visualize success prior to the walk onto the football field, through lining up the shot, to when the ball goes through the goal posts, your team rejoices and the crowd cheers. Athletes visualize successful completion as they rehearse their skills in their mind. All of the details, the emotions, the breathing are all rehearsed in minute detail. Over time, kicking that goal becomes as natural as brushing your teeth. This is called rehearsal meditation.

A good time to try this type of meditation is after going to a meeting, because it helps to have your brain in a connected and somewhat inspired or motivated place. Inventory and amends are rough tasks. Line up a light conversation or fun activity for after you do this one, especially the first time. Tell your sponsor or a buddy you're going to be doing some meditation around things in your inventory, and afterward you might want to go out and do something fun – to help change your feelings around the situation from fear and helplessness into relaxation. This will further cement the steps you have made toward feeling grounded and more self-assured. It might be a good idea to have your sponsor, or a buddy read the meditation script for you and be there with you.

WHAT YOU NEED
A pencil, and notebook: complete the following exercise on paper before you sit to meditate, it can give you several healthy, positive choices for a new direction, a new way of looking at how you act and react.

EXERCISE:
1. Think of some of your defects of character, or the things about yourself that you think may be holding you back in recovery, especially when it comes to the action in this step. For example, you may feel less than courageous when you think about facing someone who you know is very angry with you. It is hard to stand alone and vulnerable in front of someone else and admit you were wrong, then ask for forgiveness. On one page, jot down a list of the things that you think stand in the way of making amends.
2. Consider someone who you admire, who lives a quality life of recovery. Think about the attributes that you admire about them. On another page, jot down a list of things you want for your own recovery, based on what you see in this role model.
3. Consider the first person to whom you will make amends. Use your role model as an example to problem solve your approach. Jot down how your role model would handle the situation, and add your positive skills to the mix as well. Do this in as much detail as you can so that your brain has an image of you as a competent, confident, calm person

working a good recovery program with courage, compassion, strength and hope – resolving things.
- What would a person with really strong recovery do or say in this situation?
- What would a person with gratitude do or say?
- I want to handle this in the best way for the other person – what can I do to keep their feelings and interests in the front of my mind, especially once I get upset and nervous?
- If I am acting out of caring and compassion in this situation, what would it be like? How would it change? What would it feel like?

...And so on, until you have a list of things that can you could realistically use as positive actions and solutions.

When performing rehearsal meditations it helps to have a meditation "anchor" – something that connects you to something soothing, calming and light. Here's how we develop meditation anchors: Find a coin, a stone, some small object you can hold that has meaning for you. One of your AA/NA chips would be an ideal anchor! Hold it in your hand and close your eyes. Think of a time when you felt good, and bring that good feeling to the surface: the warm sun on your back when you bent to pick up the sea shell, a great cup of coffee with someone, an act of service that left you with a good feeling, the sense of belonging at a meeting. It doesn't have to be amazing; it just has to be positive. Allow yourself to sink into that positive sensation – wrap it around you and spend some time enjoying it. Smile. Touch the object as you think about the soft, positive feelings; roll it in your hand. This action helps to give us a tangible reminder of the positive feelings. We will refer back to your anchor throughout the meditation.

Find a quiet place with minimal distractions. Soft music would be helpful, with a downbeat of 60 per minute or less. The beat of music can help you to regulate your heart beat, as it works biologically, and at an unconscious level. See the back of this book where there are hints about background music.

REHEARSAL MEDITATION: THE WORST THING THAT CAN HAPPEN

We can't control the future actions of someone else. We can learn acceptance and peace through learning to allow things to just be. If we want to rehearse a situation of making amends to someone who may be very, very angry at us, we may want to rehearse how to be calm in the face of that anger. Rather than rehearsing the relationship suddenly becoming fantasy-land wonderful, we may want to rehearse how to allow the other person to keep their anger for now, and at least part ways knowing that you did your best. For many of us, acceptance requires a lot of rehearsing.

We begin:

Find a comfortable position that allows you to relax all of your muscles and still be awake.

Hold your anchor (your shell, chip, stone…) in your hand and call up the situation that you are using to bring good feelings to the present. Run your fingertips over your anchor; roll it in your hand. Beginning at your feet, imagine relaxing muscle groups with each breath: take in a relaxed, deep breath, and relax your feet and ankles. Think of that time when you felt good, and bring that good feeling to the surface as you touch your anchor.

Another deep relaxed breath, and relax your shins and calves, Allow your lower legs to relax, muscles becoming loose and soft. Take in a full deep breath. Release all tension in your lower legs.

Let it go. Think of that time when you felt good, and bring that good feeling to the surface as you touch your anchor.
Relax your thighs and hamstrings. Take in a full deep breath. Release the tension in your upper legs. Allow your hips to let go of any tension or tightness.
Take in a long deep breath: fill up your belly, your ribs, all the way to your shoulders. Breathe in until it hurts, hold it, and let it go. Think of that time when you felt good, and bring that good feeling to the surface as you touch your anchor.
Lower back and buttocks relax. Belly soft.
Chest muscles relax. Muscles between your shoulder blades relax: becoming smooth and soft. Take in a full deep breath and let it go.
Imagine your shoulders and neck muscles becoming soft, releasing all tension, all tightness, all holding. Take in a long deep breath: fill up your belly, your ribs, all the way to your shoulders. Breathe in until it hurts, hold it; and let it go. Think of that time when you felt good, and bring that good feeling to the surface as you touch your anchor.
No more tension, no more tightness, no more holding.
Allow your scalp and forehead to relax, becoming soft and smooth. The muscles of your face relax. Jaw relaxes, frown lines becoming smooth.
Take in a long deep breath: fill up your belly, your ribs, all the way to your shoulders. Breathe in until it hurts, hold it for a second and let it go. Think of that time when you felt good, and bring that good feeling to the surface as you touch your anchor. When thoughts begin wandering around in your head, bless them and let them pass.
Just watch your belly move in and out as you breathe – soft and natural. Think of that time when you felt good, and bring that good feeling to the surface as you touch your anchor.

Allow yourself to breathe slowly, softly, and naturally, and tell yourself that you are open to receive strength. Concentrate on the word "courage." Allow yourself to again touch your anchor, and sink into that positive sensation – wrap it around you and spend some time enjoying it. Smile.

Think about one of your good qualities: a beautiful smile, a caring heart, intelligence... allow yourself to feel good about that quality and sink into that as well. Enjoy good feelings for a few moments. Roll your anchor around between your fingers, feeling the texture, the weight of it as you smile. Enjoy feeling relaxed and at peace. Let the good feelings - your spirit and Higher Power - work through you.

Think of the person you will approach to make amends. Imagine preparing a list of things to say, or a letter to read to them so that your words come easier. If you feel anxiety coming, tighten every muscle in your body, stretch out your arms and legs, tighten even more, hold for a slow count of 4 and let everything go limp. Take a slow, deep breath in, and exhale. It's your choice to be calm while thinking about the situation.

What have you done to contribute to the difficulty between you and this person? What will you say to this person? Rehearse it in your mind. Imagine yourself in the situation. See all of the tiny details: Where are you? Who are you with? What are you wearing? What are you saying?

Concentrate on the word "courage." Feel the object of your anchor in your hand and bring back the positive, lighter feelings associated with it. Take a deep breath and concentrate only on staying relaxed. Try to examine this situation as if you were outside looking in. Watching a movie. Say "courage" out loud to yourself. Take a deep breath. Remember the good feelings you had a few moments ago when you recalled something good happening. Try to wrap those lighter feelings around you again.

Imagine now that you are going to the location where you will meet to make amends to this person. See the details of things around you. Imagine facing this person. Imagine your greeting, beginning your speech. Imagine the difficulty that you both will have, the awkwardness. Pause for a moment to relax: Take a slow, deep breath in, and exhale. Choose to be calm while thinking about the situation. Turn your attention to your breathing, and become more relaxed with each breath. Keep your breathing calm and slow, centered in your belly. Think of that time when you felt good, and bring that good feeling to the surface as you touch your anchor.

Imagine that the two of you begin to discuss the past. Create in your mind as much anxiety and fear as you can, and allow yourself to feel it, even though it hurts, and it's unpleasant. Feel your heart rate rise, your breath coming quicker. Tighten every muscle in your body, stretch out your arms and legs, tighten as hard as you can, hold as long as you can, let everything go limp. Take a slow, deep breath in, and exhale. Keep your breathing calm and slow, centered in your belly. Think of that time when you felt good, and bring that good feeling to the surface as you touch your anchor.

The past is over. You can look at it, but you do not have to hold on to your stress and anxiety.
You don't have to allow your fear, guilt, or shame to control you.

Imagine that as you speak, the other person begins to ask questions. Some of the questions are easy, some are difficult. Come up with many questions that you think they may have for you, answer calmly, objectively – you are there for them, not you... Take a slow, deep breath in, and exhale. Keep your breathing calm and slow, centered in your belly. Think of that time when you felt good, and bring that good feeling to the surface as you touch your anchor.

Being sorry does not guarantee forgiveness. Imagine that the other person begins to lash out in words. If you feel anxiety coming, tighten every muscle in your body, stretch out your arms and legs, tighten even more, hold for a slow count of 4 and let everything go limp. Take a slow, deep breath in, and exhale. Touch your anchor and relax your muscles. You can choose to be calm in this situation. Stand tall and listen to what they have to say. Allow them to vent. As they speak, feel compassion. Think of that time when you felt good, and bring that good feeling to the surface as you touch your anchor. No interruptions, no chiming in or excuses just listen and feel compassion for the other person. When they have finished, acknowledge their pain. Touch your anchor, trigger relaxation. Concentrate on the word "courage." No one but you can develop fear and anxiety inside of your body. That means only you can develop calm. Apologize and offer your amends.

You have imagined the worst thing that could happen, and you are okay. You have handled the situation with courage and grace. Your feelings cannot hurt you, or prevent you from doing the things you need to do. Tighten every muscle in your body, stretch out your arms and legs, tighten as hard as you can, hold as long as you can, let everything go limp. Take a slow, deep breath in, and exhale. If you have not let go of the tension, repeat.

Play the situation again briefly in your mind, and as you rehearse the outcome, feel courage, control, compassion, understanding and relaxation. Understand that no matter what the situation, you can breathe deep, choose to let go of the fear, and approach it with a calm and rational mind.

Picture the individual you were making amends to once again, and say something to your Higher Power like: "Thank you for putting _____ in my life. From _____ I am learning:_____" (list several lessons and growth opportunities you would not have, were this person not in your life.)

I can use this great opportunity to..." (name new skills and attitudes that you would like to develop to successfully resolve this situation or problem.)

The past is over. You do not have to hold stress and anxiety. You don't have to allow it to control you. Think of that time when you felt good, and bring that good feeling to the surface as you touch your anchor. Remind yourself again of your good qualities. Remind yourself of the gifts that recovery has brought to your life.

Smile, even if it's forced, and hold that smile for as long as you can. Smile until you are enjoying it. Concentrate on the words "courage and compassion." Breathe softly and deeply, and hold the smile as long as you can.

When you are ready, stretch, have a quiet cup of tea, or cool glass of water.

If you chose to do this meditation alone, call your sponsor or a buddy now. Rather than dredging up what you just went through and feeling upset all over again, go out for walk together, go somewhere light and easy, and talk about hope; feel lightness of companionship. Make a commitment to talk about it some other time. Just for a while, work hard on hugging and smiling a lot.

Through many dangers, toils and snares I have already come;
'Tis Grace that brought me safe thus far and Grace will lead me home.
-John Newton

Step 10: WORKING THE STEPS REALLY IS WORK!

Continued to take personal inventory and when we were wrong promptly admitted it

As we enter step 10, we may still not like being told when we are wrong, or that our behavior might be contributing to the stress in our lives, and/or the lives of others. Step 10 teaches us that if we want to maintain anything we have to stick to it the hardest when we want to give up the most. Recovery is not just a thing that we do – recovery has to become who we are.

The promise of this step is: Fear of people and of economic insecurity will leave us.
The lesson that this step teaches is perseverance, dedication, structure – to stick to new behaviors until personal growth becomes so much a habit that it becomes like brushing our teeth when we get up in the morning – our day would be thrown out of kilter if we didn't perform self inventory and incorporate spirituality and recovery practices.
The behaviors and attitudes that Step 10 is resolving have to do with how we incorporate honesty and judgments of others into our lives. To be human is to make mistakes. It is time to learn not to judge others but accept others for who they are, not our vision of who they should be.

WHAT YOU NEED
Read through this before you try it out. You don't have to memorize it, just get the gist of it.
If you want, record the meditation as a script and plug in the earphones as you stretch out to relax.
Weather permitting, grab a blanket and take a walk outside to your yard or a grassy area like a park or field, or a bench where

you can be undisturbed for about an hour. Bring the sunscreen, or apply before you leave.

By now you are probably feeling much more comfortable with being outside. That is a normal consequence of creating balance in your life, and using stress management techniques like meditation.

MEDITATION FOR CONNECTING TO DIVINE ENERGY: I AM SUNSHINE

One very basic goal of meditation is to teach us that the world does not stop at the boundary of our skin or thoughts. We are made of that same Divine energy as the sky, trees and our Higher Power. Spirituality/universal energy/Higher Power; and the energy of recovery are infinite. When we open our mind and heart to spiritual power, that power opens to us because there is a divine energy in the recovery process. When we begin to wonder about the miracles around us we can develop faith in that divine, creative energy, and allow it to move unrestricted through our body, mind and heart.

We begin:

If you can find a grassy place outdoors, lie flat on your back and look up at the sky, just watching the clouds floating in the sky. If you do this meditation indoors, lie flat and begin the script as if you were outside: by imagining or thinking about the images.

Search the clouds for shapes, pictures, and just consider how those clouds came to be there. Who or what made them? What put you and those clouds in the same place at this moment? Allow your thoughts to drift, and imagine your thoughts to be clouds: some heavier than others, some dark with rain, some frazzled by lightning, some filmy, some just wisps that easily dissolve into nothingness. Close your eyes and imagine your thoughts and emotions to be clouds moving across the beautiful, deep blue sky.

Begin to breathe deeply, slowly and naturally into your belly. Imagine that your body is as light as a cloud, so light that you begin to rise above the blades of grass, and begin to float upward over the trees, over the buildings and houses, toward the sky, higher…and higher. Feel yourself rocking on the breeze, floating along on the breeze as clouds do, warm and comfortable. Imagine that you can look down over the treetops, rooftops, as you float higher, leaving the stress of daily life behind.

The sun warms you from above. Think of sparkling yellow, caring, light wrapping around you, streaming into your body, energizing all of your cells. Imagine that an especially bright sunbeam is streaming into your body at the area just below where your ribs join: your diaphragm, the space where you have hiccups. Feel the sun's energy mingling with your own, increasing in warmth, strength, power.

Wonder about the sun: how did it get there? The sun is an amazing thing – what put you in this place, at this time, to enjoy it? What miracle allows you to soak in this warmth and the energy of the sun's light in this time and place? How did you and the sun come to be in this place, at this time? Allow your mind to wander and puzzle over how you got here…

Say a small intention: "Today, I will serve others. Today I will act with a caring heart."

Think of a pair of hands holding a ball of sparkling yellow energy like sunshine. Watch those hands begin to use the glowing energy like it was clay. Those hands are forming your bones, sculpting your muscles until you take shape, carving out your face, your hair from sparkling yellow light. Feel that light running through every cell of your body. Imagine that you have no skin, no boundaries. You are beautiful, sparkling sunlight: powerful, strong and warm. Picture yourself as glowing with beautiful, bright sunbeams that mingle and extend downward through the clouds - along with the other sunbeams, warming the ground, shining over everyone. Think of people that you care about, and imaging sending those sunbeams over them, warming them, sending relaxation to them from your perch in the clouds. Form an intention in your mind: "I will to do Your will. Today I will serve others. What I will do to serve is: _____."

Rest awhile, allowing yourself to float; feeling warm and peaceful in the clouds, surrounded by sunbeams. Think of those individuals in your life who you still have struggles with. Imagine that you can wrap them in sparkling sunshine, that you can soften the stress between you. One at a time, wrap them in caring light, and say a blessing for them that they might heal, that you both can find a better way.

Begin to listen to the sounds of life all around you. Wonder about what miracle allows so many people to walk, move, and work here in the same time and space… What miracles led you to be where you are right now? Think of the miracles that brought you together with people who are caring, intelligent, and creative – people who have much to share. Think about the caring of the people who you know and admire in recovery. Think about what a miracle recovery is.

Begin to feel the weight of your body again. Wonder about the grass beneath you – who or what made each tiny seed that grew into each blade? How did the ground get there? Who or what made you? How did all of it come together at once in this time and place to be surrounded by sunbeams? Think about the connection between the divine energy inside of you, the sparkling energy of the sun, blades of grass, the clouds, the earth, working a recovery program, the caring energy you feel in the rooms...

Before opening your eyes say a little prayer of thanks for this wonderful gift of peace.

Step 11: You never get voice mail when you call God

Sought through prayer and meditation to improve our conscious contact with God as we understood God, praying only for knowledge of God's will for us and the power to carry that out

In Eastern thought, spirit sends energy outward to infinity at birth, like threads. As our spiritual energy flows outward, it connects with the energy of others – so we become connected on a spiritual plane. Chinese legends describe it as the gods tying a red cord around the ankles of people that are destined to meet one another to help each other through difficult times, or as a soul mate. These are relationships that feel old when we first meet, because we feel so deeply connected on that spiritual plane.

Our mind shapes our concept of being spiritual, and our mind determines if our life is chaos and our journey is hard. When we can begin to define spirituality and spirit for ourselves, and have conscious contact with a Higher Power, the concepts of "chaos" and "hard" take on a new meaning. In step 11, through prayer and meditation, we make that contact conscious, and begin to see that the spiritual forces inside of us have been whispering in our ear all along (think of it as your Higher Power.) We now are working on how to listen. To listen to spirit, we first have to stop talking, and that includes thinking! Meditation is a great vehicle for learning to both speak to others who have wisdom, our inner spirit, and hear an answer.

As we enter step 11, we are ready to be the best we can be, to grow spiritually, but we may not really understand yet what that means. At this step we typically are still questioning why we are here, what recovery is all about, wondering what direction we should take. We understand concepts like spirituality and Higher Power through our unique creativity and imagination, which is why we all have an individualized understanding. Conscious contact with a Higher Power can also be the way in which the principles of the program speak to us and guide us through our daily tasks.

The promise of this step is: We will intuitively know how to handle situations which used to baffle us.
The lesson that this step teaches is self-reflection and spirituality. We are on a journey of healing, and recovery, and that road leads us to an understanding of our Higher Power and our spirituality, and how to bring those things to the forefront.
The behaviors and attitudes that the 11th step works on are discipline, doubt, ego, acceptance and reaching out. We will acknowledge that we don't have all the answers, and through prayer and/or conscious contact we reach out to find those answers.

WHAT YOU NEED
A nice long trail through the woods or a field. Urban trails (sidewalks) are good too if the nature paths are not accessible to you, just adapt your imagination according to what is around you.
Dress for the weather, wear comfortable walking shoes. Think about ticks, mosquitoes, loose dogs, poison ivy, and other life forms you may need to stay away from, and prepare ahead of time (based on the locality you choose.)
If you'll be in the blazing sun, cover up and get out the sunscreen.
A bottle of water would be good – we're going on a field trip. Maybe a walking stick if you have one handy or can locate one along the way – to really set the tone.

The heart is where the spirit cleanses the body of stored up emotion and history. If you think you may end the exercise on a sad note or in negativity, remember that spirit speaks to us in many ways. Feelings are not positive or negative – they simply are. Emotion is just energy going back out into the environment. Make a mental note, or leave yourself a note before you leave for your walk, to call someone to talk afterward.

Leave out a pencil and notebook to jot down your thoughts after you return home.

WALKING MEDITATION: CONNECTEDNESS
Many people feel closest to Higher Power or Divine energy in nature. Nature is filled with color, sounds, smells that are grounding. The hugeness of trees, the billions of blades of grass – the vastness of nature allows us to be humble and joyful all at once.

Beautiful things in life are often overlooked when we are stressed – we may not really see the flower that grows in the crack of the sidewalk, or the grass at our feet. Walking meditation can relieve stress and clear the mind, and you can practice it anytime, anyplace and every day. The best part is: it costs absolutely nothing! Like all meditation practices, in walking meditation the intention is to clear your mind of all thought and worry, and focus on the moment: NOW. If we can come up with nothing amazing to think about, we can at least wonder about the amazing computer system in our heads that is capable of coordinating so many systems that we can "simply" take a step. We can also think about our gratitude for being able to take a step in a world where so many cannot.

THIS IS YOUR BRAIN WALKING
In martial arts movies, we see monks walk for miles through the Himalayans without becoming tired, to beg to train in certain temples. Although these movies are stories, and we may see them as silly, walking meditation is the technique that they are illustrating. Mindful and conscious walking gives us the simple joy of being in the moment, away from problems – which allows solutions to find us. So grab a bottle of water, put on your sneakers, clear your head, and let's go outside – even a city sidewalk is an adventure!

Our goal in this meditation is to understand mindfulness. In the beginning of the book, mindfulness was described as being present only in the moment and enjoying all the sensations and experiences of that moment. Remember my dog, Cisco rummaging through the garbage, for the pork chop bone? Think of a dog happily gnawing on its' humans' shoe, or rolling in something stinky. During those moments, every cell in the dog's body is joyful, focused on the act, and present only in the moment. As we practice mindful walking meditation we want to focus on our footsteps, our breathing, what we smell, hear, see, feel, temperature, ALL of it, NOW. It takes practice. Don't worry. Most of us will have trouble reaching the level of mindfulness of a dog rolling in something stinky, but we can come very close!

NOTE FOR DOG OWNERS
If you have a dog, and want to have the dog join you, it is advisable for you to do this meditation a few times before you allow that for a couple of reasons:
- Old habits can turn this into 'walking the dog.' The goal here is for you to learn to walk yourself, and enjoy every step.
- Letting go and just enjoying everything inside and outside of your skin isn't easy. Another creature in the mix will make it too easy to become distracted from your task. A dog

suddenly yanking at a leash, or simply pulling you out of your internal space may trigger annoyance. We want positive, especially in the beginning.
- Dogs are already mindful. We need to teach you how to be mindful. Once you arrive back home from your walking meditation dancing and joyous, and can dance and celebrate with your dog just like they do at the sight of you, you have caught up to your dog in NOW ability. Once you can do that, the dog can go with you next time, and you will both have a blast rolling around, eating leaves, smelling things, chasing the wind, romping and being silly as you celebrate LIFE.

We begin:

Turn off your cell phone! OFF! Not vibrate.
Stand still for a moment, close your eyes, and listen to sounds that are around you. Try to be aware of nothing external except the sounds of life: traffic, voices, breeze blowing through trees, people working, birds, animals, the wind, horns honking. Work with what you have.
- Focus on the temperature of the air as it goes in through your nose on the inhale, and is warmed by your body as you exhale through your nose. Notice scents from flowers, foods from restaurants, exhaust from the cars, and the smell of the earth. Feel the air move against your face, on your skin. Is it cool? Warm?
- Start out at a slow, easy pace for each walking session. Think of it as strolling slowly, meandering. Avoid burning lots of calories by moving briskly.
- How you hold your body is important to walking comfortably and easily. With good posture you will be able to breathe easier and you will avoid back pain.
- Keep your elbows close to your body - don't flap like a chicken.

- Try to walk at a comfortably slow pace with intention and purpose, not simply meandering along. That means head up, shoulders up, back straight.
- Allow your hands to swing naturally with each step, not higher than your breastbone.
- The heel comes into contact with the ground first. Roll from heel to toe. Push off with the toe. Concentrate on rolling from heel to toe as you step. Keep your brain focused on your feet to keep it from reverting to its old worrying techniques.

BREATH COUNTING AND WALKING
Concentrating on the breath helps to clear the mind. Breathe through your nose for a slow count of 4 then exhale for a slow count of 4. If you are in the city, you can time your breath by telephone poles, meaning inhale the distance between poles, exhale until you reach the next one, then strive to make it longer.

WAYS TO BE MINDFUL
- Take in everything – look for things to examine, and try to be excited, respectful, in awe over twigs, stones, grass - whatever you encounter. There are so many textures, colors everywhere. Enjoy them all.
- As you begin the slow walk, turn your attention from your thoughts to your senses: do you smell things on the breeze? Are you investigating items you see on your path? Do you feel the clothes on your body? What do you hear? Allow your brain to be playful.
- Look for a treasure, something special, pick it up. Poke at it. If you are wandering in an area *and **know** the edible plants*, pick those you like the taste of and sample them.
- Collect small beautiful objects to take home, or arrange them in a temporary collage on your path: adding to the work each day for the rest of the world to also enjoy.

- Feel your feet on the ground and your balance.
- Scan your insides: any tightness, tension, pain? Are you relaxed? Can you feel the aliveness inside?
- Focus on your belly as your center, and relax the belly muscles as you walk.
- Most important of all, be honest with your self-appraisal: are you walking with intent? Confidence? Purpose? Attitude? If you are not in the moment, seeing the intent behind your movements, you are missing a deep spiritual connection between yourself, your activity and the world around you. Don't allow this to become 'just another walk!'
- Of course, your mind will wander: this is a good opportunity to cultivate patience: don't judge or trouble yourself by it, just return your attention to the movement of your body, your breathing, and the world around you. Allow the environment to distract your brain into experiencing it completely. Let your mind wonder about how many blades of grass are under your feet. If you're on a city sidewalk, wonder about how many pieces of old gum there may be – what flavor were they? Who chewed them? Who or what put you in this place, at this time to enjoy this amazing world?

BECOME COMFORTABLE IN YOUR OWN SKIN
After your walk ends, stand still, with eyes closed, and take a moment to integrate energy, peaceful attitude and insight. Open your eyes, ears, nose, skin in all directions and search for as many sounds, sights, sensations and smells as you can find. Enjoy them all. Turn your attention to your skin and just allow your brain to feel temperature, clothing, air movement. Feel each inhale as bringing relaxation and alertness to your body. Think of things to be grateful for, and as each one moves through your mind, smile and give deliberate thanks.

SECOND NOTE FOR DOG OWNERS
When you begin to incorporate the dog into mindful walking, remember: this isn't "walk the dog." It isn't fetch or Frisbee. This is a new activity. Dogs generally figure it out pretty quickly. The goal is to BE MINDFUL TOGETHER. Here's the difference: Fetch means human throws, dog gleefully bounds after, sniffs around, enjoys the chase, prances back proudly with the prize, and it happens all over again. 'YAY! I got the bouncy thing again! YAY!' The dog is having all of the fun living in the moment and rejoicing every sensation. If you were to *mindfully* fetch, the human and dog would both bound joyfully after the ball, roll around together, pick it up – tasting it, feeling the texture in our mouths, smelling the scent of the rubber or plastic (and all of the past slobber from previous fetch sessions.) Then we would together celebrate catching the prize. Together is the operative word! Here's how to mindfully join your dog in a walk: When you bring the 4 footed Zen Master with you for the first time, and you are in a place where it is safe to do so, use lots of slack in the leash. Be mindful of people, leash laws and dangers. *Have experience with your dog showing unquestionable obedience to the words: come, sit, and stay.*

Begin your time together as it directs in the script above: stand and absorb. Take a deep breath and begin to walk with intention. Allow the leash to be slack, and then allow your dog to lead YOU, and teach you about what is amazing and wonderful through their eyes as they experience their world. Watch where the dog looks, where they investigate. Investigate with the dog. When their muzzle rises to sniff the air, sniff with them and let them see and hear you doing that – be obvious about it. If you don't smell anything wonder about what it might be. When the dog finds something on the ground, look together, poke at it together, and celebrate what you have found. Find something interesting that is out of doggie reach, like a tree blossom. Take the object, hold it out and offer it for sniffing enjoyment. Sniff it together and make a joyful fuss about how wonderful it is. *If you know what it is* and it is edible by humans and canine alike, eat it together! Get excited together over sticks that are interesting to carry and carry them proudly like they are the best prize on the planet. Dance together, run and jump. Roll around on the ground.

As your walk winds down, sit somewhere comfortable where you can lean on each other. Close your eyes and breathe, enjoying NOW to the fullest. Allow leaning together to be a nice long snuggle time with hugs and kisses. Share your water bottle, and share one more dance and hug before going home.

This type of walking meditation provides human and dog with a whole new way to enjoy each other, and a spiritual bonding process like no other!

Step 12:   Servitude and gratitude

Having had a spiritual awakening as the result of these steps, we tried to carry this message to other addicts, and to practice these principles in all our affairs.

Sometimes our days are calm and uneventful, sometimes hectic and chaotic. When our day has been full of chaos, we may have trouble finding gratitude as we look back, but... Gratitude does not have to be for something earth shaking.
We can be grateful for chaos because it teaches us that we need to improve our skills for being calm.
We can be grateful for boredom, because it gives us relief from chaos.
We can be grateful for the deli man who sold us a really good cup of coffee or sandwich.
Above all, we can be grateful for the gift of each day, and for the wonderful world full of people that surround us.

When we arrive at step 12, we look back to see how much we have grown. We entered this program self-centered, isolated, selfish, afraid, thinking we were weak, and seeing no real connections between our thoughts and actions. By now we have probably figured out that when we do something only to get a reward, what we really get is anxiety, worry, and fear because we are trying to control outcomes and grab an elusive prize. When we do simply for the sake of doing, we get huge rewards, and the happiness is not as fleeting, it turns into gratitude that we can carry everywhere we go. When we offer support to others, our recovery becomes stronger: we keep what we have by giving it away. We are born to this world to serve others, grow, learn and spread joy, love, compassion and laughter.

The promise of this step is: We will suddenly realize that God is doing for us what we could not do for ourselves.
The lesson that this step teaches is servitude: our reason for being here is to serve, and service comes from unconditional love and acceptance - the highest form of spirituality.
The behaviors and attitudes that step 12 develops are community, spiritual power, the rewards of giving.

For this step we will do a listening meditation. There are listening meditations that are designed to clear our minds and hearts and bring us to gratitude. If you have a question, a thought, listening meditation can bring the answer to you. We don't typically get an answer to listening meditations in the form of words; it may come to us through feelings, intuition and circumstances. In the few days after a listening meditation we may see something in a magazine that seems to answer our question. A friend or stranger may say something out of the blue that is strangely related to what we asked. The answer may not come immediately. We don't always get an answer. Be alert for something that seems to be chance… and be careful what you ask for… remember the promise of Step 12: "…God is doing for us what we could not do for ourselves." We only need to ask. This meditation will help us to reflect a bit, and then bask in the joyful warmth of gratitude and compassion.

The more we practice this type of meditation, the more open we become to finding answers to what we seek, and the more open we are to divine energy and guidance.

To listen to spirit takes quiet, time, willingness, patience, an open mind, a closed mouth, and experimentation.

WHAT YOU NEED
Try aromas from the following, or a combination of them all:
Myrrh - spirituality, balance

Frankincense –receptivity, spiritually, meditation
Lemon - memory, clarity, spirituality, cleanses toxins.
Sweet Pea - loyalty, devotion, peace
Coconut -inner peace

LISTENING MEDITATION FOR GRATITUDE AND REFLECTION: SPEAK TO ME, SPIRIT

We all have a beast inside of us. We don't have to kill that beast or be afraid of it. We do need to see it, know it, and make peace with it, because it has touched our hearts forever. This meditation uses the image of a wolf. If you fear dogs or wolves, reflect on the skills you have been given through the program, and turn that fear over before beginning this meditation. Wolves are talismans – they represent cunning and ferocity, strength, and will power. Wolves are the pathfinders – wild, free creatures with strong, courageous spirit and the wisdom of an ancient nature.

We begin:

Find a comfortable spot. Sit with your palms resting on your legs, your back nice and straight, but not soldier-like. Be comfortable. As you breathe in, think about your body, locating any areas of tension. As you breathe out, imagine breathing out the tension into the room, until you are completely relaxed.

Breathe in, think about those areas where you had been holding on to tension lately, and imagine sending green light, and warmth to those areas one at a time. As you focus that green light on an area of your body, give thanks to it for holding your stress, try to feel compassion for the hard work those muscles have done for you, share the warmth of your smile with each area that has been working so hard to be tense. Once you feel relaxed and ready move on:

Think of yourself standing outside, at the base of a hill. At the top of the hill is a tree line. Begin walking up the hill, feeling the pleasantness of your leg muscles stretching and using energy as you climb. Off to the right, just below the tree line, you see two wolves playing. They jump and chase each other in and out of the trees, yipping in joyful tones, touching muzzles; so happy to romp in this beautiful spot. They chase each other into the trees until you can no longer see them. As you continue up the slope, your breathing becomes a little quicker, but still relaxed and deep. As you reach the hilltop and enter the trees, the temperature slowly becomes cooler. Breathe in the scents of the woods, hear birds calling to each other, feel the breeze on your skin. Feel relaxed and at peace, grateful for the chance to be in nature. Nowhere to be, nothing to do but be surrounded by the spirit of the forest.

Stop for a moment to stand in stillness in the woods, surrounded by trees. Nearby you hear a soft rustle much like leaves in the breeze. You sense someone there with you. You see a beautiful, sleek wolf, standing within an arm's length of you. You have no reason to be afraid of her. She senses your calm spirit, she sees you as part of nature. You belong in this beautiful place; as she does. She is completely serene and at peace: her ears are held back and still, her tail held low. Look into her yellow eyes. She is young, strong, and beautiful, and tall enough that you could stroke her back without bending. Her fur is shiny, tipped in silver, and it appears to be very soft. She is so close that you can see her nostrils move as she breathes in your scent, examining you. Examine her, and imagine that you can feel compassion, love, respect and ancient wisdom coming from this gentle, beautiful creature as she stands quietly with you. Feel the awe of such a courageous spirit being your companion, so close, and so at peace with you in this time and place. See the playfulness, and intelligence in her eyes... her thick, shining fur, the quiet serenity that surrounds her. Ask her: "Please, show me your favorite spot." Begin to walk on together for a while, enjoying the company of each other. The two of you come to a more open area. There is a small pool of clear water, surrounded by rock, scents of wild flowers, beautiful colors, sheltered by trees. The water is sparkling clear and cold. Sit on a rock beside the pool, and feel how the sun has warmed the rock. The rock is shaped to fit your body so perfectly that it feels like a soft, comfortable chair. Allow your fingers to reach down and touch the water. It is cold and so sparklingly clear it seems to be blue. Cup the water and take a deep drink, smiling at the coldness and sweetness of the water. The wolf lowers her head beside you to take a drink, and she laps at the cool, sweet water, enjoying it as you did.

Sit in silence on your rock; allow your eyes to close. Be still, listening to the sounds of the forest. Feel the solid rock beneath you. Feel safe, and warm, and allow your heart to feel joyful as you allow the people and things that you are grateful for to run through your mind. Your companion sits next to you, so close you can feel the warmth of her body. You are both at peace.

Open your eyes and look deep into her beautiful yellow eyes. Ask her a question, or tell her something that comes into your mind. Close your eyes again and simply wait. As you wait, focus your attention on the area around your heart; not your heart itself, but the space that surrounds it. Don't try to search for anything, don't puzzle over an answer to your question; simply sit with this beautiful, spiritual being, and wait. Open your heart, mind and ears: does she send you a message?

After waiting in silence for a few more minutes, look again into those ancient yellow eyes. She holds your gaze for a while, and then closes her eyes. She sits quietly there with you, sharing the peace, enjoying your company; her eyes closed as though she is now the one meditating, asking for answers. Close your eyes as well, and share company for a few moments, breathing in the scent of pine and earth. Look at her again: her eyes are still closed. She looks serene, relaxed. If you would like, reach out and touch her gently on the side of her muzzle. Stroke her soft fur and let her know how beautiful this moment is to you, how beautiful she is, how joyful it is to be with such a wonderful, strong, wild spirit. Thank her for sharing her time with you. As you stroke her fur, she stretches her chin up slightly, moves her head to the side, enjoying your attention. Her ears swivel slightly at the sound of a bird. Her eyes open, and make contact with yours. Her muzzle dips very slightly, almost like a nod. The wolf stands, turns and begins walking slowly, without a sound through the trees, back into the forest. When you can see her no more, close your eyes and rest.

Focus again on the area around your heart. Think of the things that happened today that came without effort, things that made you smile. Think of things that we sometimes take for granted like hot food, a soft place to sleep, the beauty of nature. Allow pictures of the wonderful people you are grateful for having in your life run through your mind, and feel a smile for each one of them as they pass through your thoughts. Take another deep, full breath of pine scented air. Form an intention to do something for someone else, yourself, nature, or your Higher Power before the day ends. Give thanks for the wonderful life you have, for your serenity and your recovery. Take 3 full deep breaths and stretch. Sit quietly for a bit before returning to your day. As you move through the rest of today, and the next few days, be alert for a sign in the environment that may be the answer to the question you asked the wolf in your meditation.

We practice these principles in all of our daily affairs...

FOR THE STILL SUFFERING: COMPASSION FOR THE HUNGRY GHOSTS

I said to my soul, be still, and wait without hope
For hope would be hope for the wrong thing; wait without love,
For love would be love of the wrong thing; there is yet faith
But the faith and the love and the hope are all in the waiting.
Wait without thought, for you are not ready for thought:
So the darkness shall be the light, and the stillness the dancing.
                                                    -T. S. Elliot

If it weren't for grace, many of us would be lost in pain and heartbreak; wondering why. In China, the Hungry Ghosts are treated with compassion. Let all of us do the same. We will end this book with meditations for the still suffering: those who have not found a path to walk out of the gates of Hell toward recovery.

Offerings for Hungry Ghosts

Many of us like to perform rituals or ceremonies to keep us in touch with something we're working on. Ceremonies and rituals are great ways to celebrate life. Ceremonies can help to bring our compassion and gratitude to the front of our minds, which over time influences our overall outlook on life. There is something nice about a meditative practice that is filled with symbolism, which you can hold in your hand, and also practice with others. Below is an offering meditation and ritual that you can practice each day, much like saying "grace" as you sit for a meal. It will keep the hungry ghost in you, and in those you know, at the front of your mind, and provide a nice way to pay tribute and to honor them.

Buddhism teaches that we all frequent the Realm of Desire: the place where we wait for reincarnation, with the goal of coming back as a higher form until we reach the state of heavenly being, or angels. The Realm of Desire has six levels of beings in it:
1. Hell beings, who cultivated anger and hatred in life.
2. Hungry ghosts, our gaki, with endless hunger and thirst.
3. Animals.
4. Humans.
5. Asuras – who during life may have had good intentions, but committed acts of jealousy, harm or agression toward others.
6. Heavenly beings – using up their good karma in the realm of bliss.

Several religions and cultures provide us with ceremonies to send out good energy and prayers for beings who are lower on the spiritual scale than we are: animals, hungry ghosts, and hell beings. The ceremony that follows is a food blessing to relieve the suffering of the hungry ghosts so they can eat and drink with "normal" people. You can do this alone, with family and friends, or during parties and feasts for holidays.   It is similar to what you might do during the Feast for the Hungry Ghosts in China.

THE RITUAL
You can vary this to what suits you:
- In China it is typical to set a place at the table, and bless food on behalf of hungry ghosts as you sit for your own meal; so essentially, there is a guest at the table that no one can see.

The offering is typically a few grains of rice or food in tiny quantities. Remember: gaki have tiny little mouths, so the portions need to be just a little tidbit.
- If friends and family are present, you can pass a bowl around, and each person contributes a tiny bite of their meal, and a few drops of whatever they are drinking.

As you begin to put food and drink into the bowl, give a blessing: "As long as I (we) live, please allow me (us) to relieve the pain of others through love and respect, and feel compassion for those who still suffer. This food and drink is offered for a hungry ghost. [If you are offering on behalf of an actual person who has passed, give their name here.] I (we) ask that you sit with us for our meal, and are able to enjoy this food and drink as we all do. We wish you peace."

Allow the bowl to sit at a place on the table you as you finish your meal. After the meal, if you are in a place where you can do this, put your offering outside on the ground where it can feed birds, squirrels, "wild life." If giving the food back to nature isn't feasible, throw it away.

MEDITATION FOR COMPASSION: GIVE AND TAKE

The meditation that follows is based in the Tibetan style called Tonglen, which loosely translates to: sending and receiving. In most of the meditations we have done together, we have focused on a way to make pain and stress turn into relaxation. Tonglen teaches us how to take on the suffering of others in a selfless way, which in turn, increases our compassion and love for all people. Selfless acts put an end to selfishness. Tonglen also speaks to continuing to keep our memory green by staying in touch with our own internal pain and fear on a continual basis, and giving compassion to our self, because we cannot give compassion to others if we don't have it for ourselves. I realize that doesn't really sound attractive and relaxing; like something you'd now want to run out and try. Please trust in ancient techniques one more time, and understand that compassion really originates in our ability to walk in another's shoes. To do that we have to know pain. This meditation sounds unpleasant by description, but with faith you will find that the reverse is true. Practice of Tonglen will leave you in peace, result in a stronger appreciation and love for other people, and a sense of how you fit into the universe. We are born to give, and nothing makes a human happier.

Within this meditation, there is the action of tapping the area over the heart. Although my meditation teacher was Hindu, and Tonglen is Tibetan, she taught us that the energy centers of our body open wider and faster when we tap or massage those areas as we focus on them. The energy of the area around the heart is the energy of love, compassion and healing. Tonglen speaks of absorbing into the heart area, so tapping the breast bone with our fingers accelerates the cleansing of that area, and is symbolic of pushing love and compassion into the heart. In meditation class, whenever we learned meditations related to compassion we were taught to tap that area, because compassion and love is something we need a lot more of in this world.

As you work through this, allow yourself the freedom to fight against something that can ultimately bring you to peace. Allow your brain to say "I'm tired of tapping on my chest – just paying attention will work just as well..." Use that kind of resistance as part of the pain that you will explore in Tonglen meditation. Letting go to do things we don't know about, and are unfamiliar with can be creepy and strange. Change is hard. Growth hurts. Recovery is worth it.

Here's a sample of how Tonglen works: if you know someone who is ill, or hurting, see them in your mind, look at their picture, or see them in person. Really look at them. Try to put yourself in their place. What do you think you would you feel? How would you react? What do you think is happening in their body, mind, and spirit? See their pain as black smoke surrounding them. Ask to be able to take that darkness from them: Try to feel what they feel. What would comfort you if you were in this situation? As you breathe in, ask your Higher Power to take away the pain from their body, mind and spirit and allow you to take it. Imagine that you are breathing in their hurt and suffering in the form of black smoke. As you exhale, imagine that you are sending them compassion, healing light or energy, recovery, relaxation: anything that you might want if you were them.

It is natural to resist or run from pain and discomfort. It can be frightening to think in terms of taking on the pain of others. This type of meditation goes back hundreds of years, and is specific to the development of a loving outlook on life. To have something of value, like recovery, we have to explore the pain within it, and find acceptance. Tonglen is one way to find that acceptance. 12 Step Programs teach us that what we resist persists. We will start our meditation by looking at what we are feeling, then progress to include others.

We Begin:

Lie back, closing your eyes. Take deep, slow breaths and use your exhale to let go, and release any tension that you may be holding on to.
Focus on your feet, relax the tension in your feet.
Relax your calves. Allow your lower legs to relax, muscles becoming loose and soft. Take in a full deep breath. Release the tension in your lower legs, and let go.

Relax your thighs and hamstrings. Take in a full deep breath. Release the tension in your upper legs. Allow your hips to let go of tension or tightness.

Take in a long deep breath: fill up your belly, your ribs, all the way to your shoulders. Breathe in until it hurts, hold it for a second and let it go.

Lower back and buttocks relax. Belly soft.

Chest muscles relax. Muscles between your shoulder blades relax, becoming smooth and soft. Take in a full deep breath and let it go.

Imagine your shoulders and neck muscles becoming soft, releasing all tension, all tightness, all holding. Take in a long deep breath: fill up your belly, your ribs, all the way to your shoulders. Breathe in until it hurts, hold it for a second and let it go.

No more tension, no more tightness, no more holding.

Allow your scalp and forehead to relax, becoming soft and smooth. The muscles of your face relax. Jaw relaxes, frown lines becoming smooth.

Take in a long deep breath: fill up your belly, your ribs, all the way to your shoulders. Breathe in until it hurts, hold it for a second and let it go.

When thoughts begin wandering around in your head, bless them and let them pass.

Just watch your belly move in and out as you breathe – soft and natural.

As thoughts enter your mind, allow them to come and go.

Bring a memory to your mind of the darkness that lives inside of you. Remember the feelings of pain in your body, mind, and spirit. Bring the darkness inside of you to life by imagining that it is made of swirling black smoke. Imagine that the smoke takes a dark and somewhat human form. It sits facing you on a chair.

Ask your dark self:

"What do you see?

What do you hear?

How do you feel inside?
What would give you some comfort?
What do you need?"

Imagine stretching your hands out toward your dark self with your palms turned upward, and absorbing swirling black smoke through the palms of your hands. AS you absorb the smoke, turn your attention inside: do you notice physical sensations? Is your stomach tight? Jaw clenched? Feelings are energy. Feelings are how we choose to interpret something that happens to us. Feelings can be changed.

Remember the many things that you have done to get your feet on the road to wellness and a more spiritual life. As you continue to breathe in the swirling black cloud of smoke, say to your dark self: "Please, let me take this pain from you, so you can be well. I want to give you peace." Breathe in slowly and deeply, and imagine that the black smoke enters your nostrils as you inhale, and flows down toward your heart. As the smoke enters the area around your heart it dissolves. Say: "To feel your pain is a gift."

Breathe in all of the shame, anger, fear, and allow it to dissolve as it enters the area near your heart. Say: "I want to send you healing, tell me what you need."

Take a long, deep breath: breathe in until it hurts, hold it for a second, and imagine that as you breathe out, you are sending yourself caring, compassion, relief, joy, warmth... Reach out your hands, and offer to lead your dark self to a path that will end in healing.

Take in a long deep breath: this time imagine that you are breathing in the dark, smoke of pain from everyone in the world who has ever felt pain like this. Fill up your belly, your ribs, all the way to your shoulders. Breathe in until it hurts, hold it for a second, imagining that you can breathe out relief for that pain, and exhale. Take in another long deep breath and as you exhale, feel compassion, love, joy, serenity, and send those positive feelings out to all who still suffer, including yourself. Say: "I recognize hunger. I know pain. Please let me lighten the burden for all people who still suffer. Please let me give them strength and hope."

Allow the images to fade. Sit in stillness for a moment. Allow thoughts to pass. Turn your attention to your solar plexus: the area where you have hiccups. Imagine that there is a glowing ball of yellow energy in this spot: warm, sparkling light like sunshine. Imagine that with each inhale that energy flows upward through the top of your head, and begins to melt down all around you until you are glowing, as if you have been back-lit by sunshine. Take a few deep natural breaths, breathing in peace and stillness, deliberately relaxing muscles, exhaling any tension as you bring that yellow energy up through the top of your head, allowing it to flow downward all around you, calming your emotions and quieting your mind. As the beautiful yellow light completely surrounds you, think of it as being your inner spiritual energy. See yourself as a shining, beautiful being made of nothing but that warm yellow light.

Breathe in until it hurts, as you exhale, take three fingers of one hand and begin to tap on your breast bone: the armor that covers your heart. Imagine that an emerald green, glowing ball of light forms in the space around your heart. Allow your fingers to strike heavily, firmly, and pause between taps. Set your own rhythm, allow yourself to think about things that still hurt you, and allow yourself to feel your pain and fear. Imagine that each tap is opening your heart. As you tap and push in what hurts, think of each hurt melting away in the healing green ball of energy that surrounds your heart. Anger, dissolves into love. Feeling unsafe turns into feeling powerful and confident in the beautiful green light; shame turns into healing as it dissolves. Let it all into your heart and watch it melt away, being transformed into the positive side of the emotion or situation. Imagine as you push in more and more pain and sadness, the armor covering your chest crumbles away and beautiful, glowing, green light bursts out, radiating all around you.

As you keep tapping your fingers, heavy on your chest, turn your thoughts to experiences of gratitude and acts of kindness that were gifts to you from friends, family, people in the program, random strangers... Focus on those acts of kindness one at a time and relive the feelings, and the types of support each person gave to you. Smile for each of those gifts. Tap and push gratitude and smiles into your heart. The area where you used to store your pain begins to turn into your center for healing.

With each exhale, think of deep green light coming from your heart area, radiating outward in all directions, touching on people you know who suffer, especially those who you may have difficult or strained relationships with. Try to actually bring up healing sensations: joy, compassion, love, laughter, peace... and send them outward to each of them with your breath. Send them healing green light and give thanks for having them in your life, to teach you lessons. Ask to send them the gift of peace and healing. When you can think of no more people, stop tapping, and allow your hand to rest in your lap as you breathe deeply and naturally. Form an intention in your mind: "Difficult people are suffering. When I meet people who suffer I will picture their pain as black smoke. I will ask to take in the darkness for them, so they can be free. As I take their darkness I will breathe out compassion, joy, understanding and acceptance. I will ask that we all be healed."

Form an intention to do something for someone else, yourself, nature, or your Higher Power before the day ends. Give thanks for the wonderful life you have, for your serenity. Take 3 full deep breaths and stretch. Sit quietly for a bit before returning to your day.

As you move through the rest of the day, when you find yourself in a difficult situation, breathe in the darkness of the situation, bring up compassion and joy to wish on the situation, and ask for healing.

AMBIANCE: SCENT, SOUND, AND MAKING YOUR OWN TAPES

MAKING YOUR OWN TAPES

It can be fun to give paper to friends and have them each write an image, and then combine several to make one script. You'll want your scripts to be detailed but not overly complicated. Incorporate the senses. Try to engage the mind in being curious. If the script triggers strong emotions, put in something soothing so that the emotional state doesn't remain raw.

Below are some notes to help you to record your own scenes for meditation.

- Pause frequently to allow time for reflection or imaging. A good way to gauge how long to pause is to read a sentence out loud, then perform the action yourself. Add a couple of additional seconds for good measure.
- For deep breathing, each inhale should last a slow count of 4, the exhales a slow count of 4 (one Mississippi, two Mississippi...). Pause a moment longer before reading on.
- If a section of the image is directing you to wait and consider, or sit in stillness, 10 full seconds is about the shortest pause you may want. It seems like a long time when you are making a tape, but when you are doing the meditation, you'll need time for your mind to wander, consider, learn, image, etc.
- Don't concentrate on saying each word clearly and distinctly; it will sound artificial and be a distraction when you are listening to it play back. Speak naturally, but at a slightly slower pace.

- Use music in the background as you record for an added boost. Music for relaxation should have 60 beats per minute or less – your heart rhythm will synchronize with the downbeat, so slow is good.

All guided images have the same components:
1. entering relaxation, typically focusing on progressive muscle relaxation, or counting backward.
2. finding a safe place, the beach, the woods, somewhere beautiful and full of sights and sounds – involve all senses.
3. undoing something negative/performing something positive, this isn't as hard to do as you might think – create an image that has to do with handing things over, listening to wisdom, etc
4. returning to conscious state from the safe place.

Below are some hints for how to put all of that together:
The "deep relaxation" part:
"Sit comfortably, feet flat on the floor, hands resting palms down on your legs…. " (PAUSE about 3 seconds for silence) "Breathe deeply into your belly. Inhale…" (count 5 slow seconds for silence) "and exhale…" (count 5 slow seconds for silence)
 - continue with your relaxation exercises by either using Progressive Relaxation or another method to give time to unwind.

The "safe place" part:
"Imagine that you stand up and begin walking …" (describe details of a scene – beach, walking in a cornfield, etc. PAUSE for about 10 seconds) "It's a warm summer day. Feel the sun on your skin. Feel a breeze ruffle your hair, and the thin hairs on your arms…" (PAUSE at least 10 seconds) "Listen to the birds.
- continue with images that create a pleasant, peaceful place.

The "performing something positive" part:
"As you walk, go back to an experience that you had today that made you smile. If you had a bad day, go back to another time when something made you laugh, or made you feel really warm and happy... " (PAUSE 10 SECONDS) "Just take that feeling, and wrap it around yourself. Enjoy it again, intensify it and fill every cell of your body with that feeling..." -then continue with an image that will provide resolution to stress, something worrying you, etc.)

Returning to conscious state from the safe place part:
"Take a deep breath, turn slowly, and begin to walk back the way you came..." (PAUSE about 10 seconds) "The sun is beginning to go down, and you feel a coolness in the air. Just concentrate on the feeling of the cooler breeze on your skin as you walk. Relaxed, carefree and light...
It is generally good to end a meditation by grounding, meaning bringing a person back to planet earth: "Wiggle your fingers and toes and give yourself a big cat stretch..."

USING ESSENTIAL OILS TO ENHANCE MEDITATION

Essential oils are concentrated extracts taken from the roots, leaves, seeds, or blossoms of plants. Some oils promote physical healing, others effect emotion and mood, some are calming, some energizing. You should never take essential oils by mouth unless you are under the supervision of a trained professional. Some oils are toxic, and taking them by mouth could be fatal. Rarely, essential oils can induce side effects when diffused into the air or put on the skin: rash, headache, as well as harm to a fetus are possible, so individuals who may be sensitive, prone to allergy, pregnant – or nursing, should not use essential oils unless approved by their doctor.

They are called "essential" oils because they are oils extracted from the bark, blossom, or other part of the plant – but the oil is what gives the plant its aroma – it's "essence." They are not always 'oily' to the touch, but they are concentrated, and very potent. If you are new to the world of essential oils, go to a good "mom and pop" type of health food store and check out the display.

You can burn essential oils by adding a few drops in a candle, or by using a diffuser. Diffusers can generally be purchased in the same health food store where you find your oils. Oils can also be diluted and used in a spray bottle, or roll on application if they are suitable for use on the skin. Look for information about each scent: there should be hard copies of lists they can give to you, or a chart on the wall. Talk to the shop owner about how best to dilute the oils the shop sells: different brands may dilute differently, or they may already be diluted, allowing you to spray or test it on your skin. If the shop staff don't appear knowledgeable, go to another store.

SCENT FOR A PURPOSE
It would be a good idea to check out how to make combinations of oils on the Internet. There are many recipes. Up to 5 oils at a time can be combined to bring out certain moods. Select a scent for a particular purpose: for instance, lavender is known for calming effects.

Test your own sensitivity first by smelling the oil: you will have an adverse reaction to scents that aren't meant for you. If you want to use one in the stress reduction category, but when you sniff lavender and think 'yuck!' it's not the one for you —go for another in the calming category like chamomile. If you want to combine some, choose the effect that you want to create and sniff samples, choosing the ones that appeal to you the most. Avoid buying lots of different oils that you haven't smelled first.

The easiest way to use oils for meditation is to put some on a napkin, and sit it near enough to smell it.

If you have pets, be aware that what you find calming and soothing may not be to their liking, so just as you sniffed to determine if it was pleasing, they should have that opportunity. Never present a bottle directly to an animal's nose! Animals have a much stronger sense of smell and sensitivity to essential oil effects. As you tested for your own adverse reaction, allow your pet to sniff from a distance. You might cup your hand around the top so that they can smell it through your fingers but not get too close to the open bottle. If they turn away, sneeze or shake their heads, you may want to exclude them from the area until your meditation atmosphere dissipates, or choose something else. Eventually, locate scents that they enjoy as well and make it a well-rounded experience.

Yea, when this flesh and heart shall fail, and mortal life shall cease,
I shall possess within the veil, a life of joy and peace.
-John Newton

Thank you to all who lent hand, heart and support to this book.

I have been blessed to have so many amazing teachers in my lifetime... most of them were my students.

May you always know peace.

CITATIONS

Amazing Grace lyrics; John Newton (1725-1807); constitution.org/col/amazing_grace

The 12 Steps and the 12 Promises are from the Big Book of AA.

Supernatural beings in Chinese folklore: Wikipedia

Clip Art and photos: Office at Microsoft on line. Photo of man and dog by Kathryn Bedard.

Tree lore: www.helium.com/items/967484-tree-lore-and-the-significance-of-different-types-of-trees

Quote: "Believing that we are being cared for is a result of developing a relationship with a Power greater than ourselves." Pg 53, Narcotics Anonymous: It Works, How and Why: The Twelve Steps and Twelve Traditions of Narcotics Anonymous (electronic large print edition, c2003) (PDF at na.org)

Quote: "... practice these principles in all our affairs." Twelve Steps and Twelve Traditions, p. 106

Quote: T. S. Elliot, The Four Quartets, Harcourt Publishing, 1943; www.tristan.icom43.net

Cover art: Gaki Zoshi (Scroll of the Hungry Ghosts) Heian Period. Tokyo Museum
http://www.tnm.jp/uploads/r_collection/LL_C0016937.jpg

See also:
Kathryn Bedard; *Stones In My Heart Forever 9-11: A Journey Through Courage, Strength and Hope.* 2008, ISBN: 9781434376152 AuthorHouse.

Made in the USA
Monee, IL
16 December 2023

49556873R00102